CONTENTS

PEACE CORPS/HONDURAS
HISTORY AND PROGRAMS

History of the Peace Corps in Honduras

Times have changed since the First Lady Doña Alejandrina Bermudez de Villeda Morales accompanied the first training class of Peace Corps Volunteers to Honduras in 1962. Over the past 40+ years, more than 5,000 Volunteers have served in Honduras in a wide range of project areas, including health, fisheries, beekeeping, animal husbandry, special education, vocational education, small business, and agriculture. Project areas and the number of Volunteers have changed in response to the changing needs of the country. Projects such as fisheries, beekeeping, and education were phased out as Honduran people and institutions developed the capacity to continue the work on their own. Other projects, such as municipal development, HIV/AIDS prevention, and business development, have been initiated or have evolved with technological advances, increased globalization of world markets, and other developments.

In response to the crisis caused by Hurricane Mitch in 1998, the number of Volunteers in Honduras increased dramatically, and in the early 2000s there were approximately 225 Volunteers. Today an average of 180 to 200 Volunteers work throughout Honduras, except in the Bay Islands and La Mosquitia.

History and Future of Peace Corps Programming in Honduras

The Peace Corps/Honduras program has six primary projects: business development, child survival and HIV/AIDS prevention, water and sanitation, protected areas management, youth development, and municipal development. We collaborate with the government of Honduras, Honduran and international nongovernmental organizations (NGOs), and communities throughout the country. Our program works in concert with the poverty-reduction strategy developed by Honduras and the international donor community. This type of integrated community development program makes Peace Corps/Honduras a traditional post in many ways. Community development and integrated rural development have been around conceptually for at least 40 years and were especially popular from the mid-1960s until about the late 1970s. We all have learned a lot since then about human capital, social capital, dependency and empowerment, and sustainability. We know that development takes a long time, with consistent work in an auspicious setting, which we do our best to provide through excellent site selection. Despite the traditional appearance, Peace Corps/Honduras' approach to, and work in, HIV/AIDS prevention, municipal development, business and information technology, protected areas management, and youth development put us very much in the vanguard of Peace Corps programming worldwide. Our objective as community development facilitators is not to teach the people of Honduras "American" values but to help them help themselves within their own cultural framework.

The health project focuses on HIV/AIDS education and prevention, child survival, and reproductive health. The water and sanitation project provides technical assistance for constructing water supply and waste management systems. At the same time, the project empowers communities to manage their water systems and protect their watersheds by developing water boards in conjunction with municipal environment committees. The protected areas management project focuses on agroforestry and natural resource management in buffer-zone communities. Business development Volunteers apply basic business skills to help organizations and entrepreneurs better utilize local resources to increase income and opportunity. Municipal development Volunteers work with municipal employees and community leaders to improve access to public services, increase citizen participation, and enhance civic education. Finally, the youth development project focuses its work with youth, parents, and teachers. It builds on existing cross-project efforts, leadership development, gender equality, education, and increasing opportunities for Honduran youth.

Peace Corps/Honduras emphasizes cross-project collaboration. Volunteers are likely to find themselves sharing or coordinating projects with Volunteers from other sectors. Additionally, Peace Corps/Honduras has taken a number of initiatives to enrich projects and allow for increased opportunity in community development. These initiatives include gender inclusion and development, environmental education, cross-project youth development, HIV/AIDS prevention, and information and communication technology.

COUNTRY OVERVIEW: HONDURAS AT A GLANCE

History

Human occupation of what is now Honduras began between 9000 and 7000 B.C. These original inhabitants were nomadic hunters. Agriculture in the region began about 6,000 years ago, when people began to gather in villages. The Maya Indians settled in western Honduras around 1000 B.C. and developed an important network of communities centered around the city of Copán. Archaeological remains tell the story of a civilization that grew slowly from 2000 B.C. to A.D. 800, greatly expanded, and then collapsed around A.D. 900. The civilization's descendants, the Maya Chortí, inhabit the region today.

The European invasion of Honduras began in 1502 with the fourth and last voyage of Christopher Columbus. He arrived on the island of Guanaja, which he called *Isla de Pinos* (Pine Island). Before the arrival of the Spaniards, Honduras was heavily populated with an estimated 500,000 to 1 million people. However, slavery and diseases (e.g., smallpox) diminished the population to fewer than 20,000 in less than 100 years.

Additional Spanish expeditions to Honduras occurred in 1524 and 1525, including one from Mexico commanded by Hernán Cortés. The occupiers appointed a governor, but the native population of Lenca Indians would not accept colonialism without a war. Lempira, the chief of the Lencas, led 30,000 Indians against the Spaniards on several occasions until 1536. During peace talks, he was betrayed and assassinated, and Indian resistance was quickly suffocated. The Spanish colonization brought not only new kinds of people—from Spaniards to African slaves—but also new species of plants and animals. The Spaniards introduced cattle and horses to the New World and took tobacco, coffee, maize, potatoes, and cacao to the Old World. In time, gold and silver mining techniques were introduced, large cattle ranches and plantations were developed, and new towns and fields emerged from the forests.

Central America gained its independence from Spain in 1821, and within a short time various factions developed. During this period, Central America was briefly annexed to Mexico, and then withdrew to join the newly formed United Provinces of Central America. However, conservative politicians in the Central American government who rejected the plan invaded Honduras in 1826. Francisco Morazán, a liberal, repelled the invasion and took control, but efforts to maintain the union were unsuccessful. In 1838, the countries decided to go their separate ways. Honduras signed a new constitution in 1839. Its first capital was Comayagua. In 1880, President Marco Aurelio Soto moved the capital to Tegucigalpa, in part because his Guatemalan Indian wife was not accepted by the high society of Comayagua. Another factor in the rise of Tegucigalpa was its great mineral wealth of gold and silver.

Since independence, Honduras has suffered nearly 300 internal rebellions, civil wars, *coups d'état*, and changes of government, more than half of which took place during the 20th century. The country has also been the target of foreign intervention, the most famous being that of U.S. soldier William Walker, who appointed himself president of Nicaragua in 1860 and aimed to take over the rest of Central America. His campaign ended in failure, and he was executed in Trujillo.

As a result of its infamous banana companies and "banana wars," Honduras was known as the Banana Republic. When banana production dominated the economy, these companies had great influence in local politics. In 1913, for example, the Standard Fruit Company and the Cuyamel Fruit Company owned 75 percent of the nation's banana plantations and nearly 100 percent of its politicians. While the banana companies built railroads and seaports, little of their wealth remained in Honduras.

Government

Honduras' governmental structure is similar to that of the United States. The Constitution of 1982 provides for a strong executive branch, a unicameral National Congress elected by popular vote, a judiciary branch appointed by the National Congress, and a president elected to a four-year term by popular vote. Since 1980, the country has had seven general elections.

In November 2009 Porfirio Lobo Sosa from the National Party was elected as president (see "Online Articles" section for link to information about the Honduran political crisis of 2009); he will hold the office until January 2014. The 128 members of the National Congress are also elected for a four-year term. Congressional seats are assigned to a party's candidate in proportion to the number of votes received by each party during the election process. The National Party has 71 Congress representatives, the Liberal Party has 45, the Christian Democrat Party has five, the Unified Democrat Party has four, and the Innovative and Unified Party of Honduras has three representatives.

Honduras is divided into 18 departments (states), each with its own *cabecera departamental* (capital). Municipal authorities are also elected for four years during general elections.

The judicial branch includes a Supreme Court of Justice, courts of appeal, and several courts of original jurisdiction, such as labor and criminal courts. The executive branch consists of 16 Secretariats: Government and Justice, Defense, Finance, Education, Health, Labor, Communications and Public Works, Natural Resources, Sports, Culture and Arts, Tourism, Presidency, Foreign Relations, Commerce and Industry, Agriculture and Live Stock, and Technical and International Cooperation.

Economy

Agriculture and forestry are the largest sectors in the economy, providing 60 percent of all jobs and two-thirds of the nation's exports. The major products for export are timber, bananas, meat, and coffee. Their production usually involves foreign capital and is highly developed. While *campesinos* (small farmers) constitute the social majority, their contribution to the gross national product (GNP) is minor because they still rely on traditional agricultural practices, including slash-and-burn cultivation and the use of wooden plows. Coffee and bananas contribute more than 50 percent of the country's export revenues. In addition, nontraditional exports such as shrimp and lobster have begun to impact the economy.

Maquiladoras, or factories, that assemble imported items for re-export were introduced in 1990 to take advantage of the country's low wages (which range from $2 to $3 per day in the non-export agricultural sector to as much as $4 per day in the export sector). The Honduran *maquiladoras* have earned a negative reputation in the United States because of adverse publicity about their use of child labor. In most *maquiladoras*, the workers are young women, often single mothers who support their families with low but sufficient wages. It is estimated that 80 percent of men ages 18 to 25 are unemployed.

In the 1980s, the United States gave aid money to Honduras for the use of its territory in support of the Contras' efforts to overthrow the Sandinistas in Nicaragua. Most of the aid money was spent on supporting the Contras rather than on the country's vast social needs. Through overspending, the Honduran government eventually amassed a huge fiscal deficit, and because of its debt, international banks cut off financing.

Honduras' economic situation remains uncertain. In 1994, a drought resulted in a shortage of electric power. In 1998, Hurricane Mitch devastated numerous rural and urban areas, many of which have yet to be fully reconstructed. While international disaster relief funds helped Honduras during this crisis, they made little impact in the fight against poverty. Most of these funding sources were exhausted in 2002.

Honduras is the second poorest country in Central America, with an unequal distribution of income and, as such, the country suffers from high crime, frequent labor strikes, and high unemployment. Unemployment increased after the approval of a new minimum wage law in late 2008. The law has resulted in some businessmen letting go of some of their employees, claiming they could not pay the new salary. In March 2005, Honduras became the second country to ratify the U.S. Central American Free Trade Agreement (CAFTA) in the hopes that expanding trade will increase job growth.

People and Culture

The majority of the population is a mixture of indigenous, African, and Spanish heritage sometimes referred to as *Ladino*. There are minorities of Europeans, Africans, Asians, and Arabs and six main indigenous groups: the Miskito, Pech (or Paya), Maya Chortí, Lenca, Jicaque (or Tolupan), and Tawahka. Another group in this diverse mix is the Garifuna. In the 1500s, when Europeans brought African slaves to the Caribbean islands, the slaves on two ships that wrecked near St. Vincent escaped. The Africans adopted the language and culture of their hosts, the Carib Indians, and intermarriage resulted in a group known today as the Garifuna, or black Caribs. In 1700, Britain took over St. Vincent, and in 1797 the Garifuna were exiled to the island of Roatán. They later spread to Belize, Nicaragua, and other parts of Honduras.

Most Hondurans are Roman Catholic, but Protestant congregations do exist in fewer numbers. Although Spanish is the predominant language, some people, especially along the north coast and in the Bay Islands, speak English. Garifuna is spoken in Garifuna communities.

The country has an estimated population of 7.3 million people and enjoys a relatively low population density, especially compared with neighboring El Salvador and Guatemala. On the other hand, its population distribution and growth patterns are not favorable. The area suitable for settlement is limited, so the bulk of the population is concentrated in the city of Tegucigalpa, the Comayagua and San Pedro Sula valleys, and the north coast. The eastern quadrant of the country remains one of the most inaccessible and least inhabited areas of Central America. The rate of annual population growth was estimated at 2.024 percent in 2008. Rapid population growth is placing increasing strains on the government's capacity to keep pace in providing health, economic, educational, and other services to the Honduran people.

Environment

With a land area of 44,997 square miles (112,492 square kilometers), Honduras is the second largest country in

Central America. The climate is characterized by a wet season from June to November and a dry season from December to May. Climatic variations are more pronounced in the coastal lowlands, particularly in the north, where major hurricanes and severe floods and droughts have occurred in recent years. Temperate conditions prevail in the higher elevations.

The country consists of mountains, mangrove and other forests, beaches, and coral reefs. It has more than 500 miles of exceptional coastline. Two-thirds of the terrain is mountainous, with agriculture and small cities tucked away in valleys. The average altitude is 1,000 feet above sea level, with the highest peak, in Celaque National Park, reaching 9,275 feet.

Honduras also possesses an underwater paradise of coral reefs on the Caribbean coast, the longest in the Northern Hemisphere, which is easily accessible from the Bay Islands. About 45 percent of the land is covered with forests. Among the tree species are palm, pine, mahogany, Spanish cedar, balsa, and rosewood. Honduras is home to several distinct ecosystems, including lowland rain forests and highland cloud forests in the interior, tropical rain forests on the Atlantic coast, and dry forests on the Pacific coast.

RESOURCES FOR FURTHER INFORMATION

Following is a list of websites for additional information about the Peace Corps and Honduras and to connect you to returned Volunteers and other invitees. Please keep in mind that although we try to make sure all these links are active and current, we cannot guarantee it. If you do not have access to the Internet, visit your local library. Libraries offer free Internet usage and often let you print information to take home.

A note of caution: As you surf the Internet, be aware that you may find bulletin boards and chat rooms in which people are free to express opinions about the Peace Corps based on their own experience, including comments by those who were unhappy with their choice to serve in the Peace Corps. These opinions are not those of the Peace Corps or the U.S. government, and we hope you will keep in mind that no two people experience their service in the same way.

General Information About Honduras

www.countrywatch.com/
On this site, you can learn anything from what time it is in the capital of Tegucigalpa to how to convert from the dollar to the lempira. Just click on Honduras and go from there.

www.lonelyplanet.com/destinations
Visit this site for general travel advice about almost any country in the world.

www.state.gov
The State Department's website issues background notes periodically about countries around the world. Find Honduras and learn more about its social and political history. You can also go to the site's international travel section to check on conditions that may affect your safety.

www.psr.keele.ac.uk/official.htm
This includes links to all the official sites for governments worldwide.

www.geography.about.com/library/maps/blindex.htm
This online world atlas includes maps and geographical information, and each country page contains links to other sites, such as the Library of Congress, that contain comprehensive historical, social, and political background.

www.cyberschoolbus.un.org/infonation/info.asp
This United Nations site allows you to search for statistical information for member states of the U.N.

www.worldinformation.com
This site provides an additional source of current and historical information about countries around the world.

Connect With Returned Volunteers and Other Invitees

www.rpcv.org
This is the site of the National Peace Corps Association, made up of returned Volunteers. On this site you can find links to all the Web pages of the "Friends of" groups for most countries of service, comprised of former Volunteers who served in those countries. There are also regional groups that frequently get together for social events and local volunteer activities.

This site is hosted by a group of returned Volunteer writers. It is a monthly online publication of essays and Volunteer accounts of their Peace Corps service.

Online Articles/Current News Sites About Honduras

http://en.wikipedia.org/wiki/2009_Honduran_constitutional_crisis

An exhaustive article on the political events of 2009 in Honduras. Highly recommended.

www.honduras.net

A Honduran Web portal with a variety of resources.

www.marrder.com/htw

Online version of *Honduras This Week*, an English-language weekly newspaper.

www.hondudata.com

General information about Honduras (in Spanish).

Recommended Books

1. Acker, Alison. *Honduras: The Making of a Banana Republic*. Cambridge, Mass.: South End Press, 1989.

2. Alvarado, Elvia. *Don't Be Afraid, Gringo: A Honduran Woman Speaks From the Heart (The Story of Elvia Alvarado)*. New York: HarperCollins, 1989.

3. Amaya Amador, Ramón. *Prisión Verde (Green Prison)*. Tegucigalpa, Honduras: Editorial Universitaria, Universidad Nacional Autonoma de Honduras, 1987. (In Spanish)

4. Berryman, Phillip. *Inside Central America: The Essential Facts Past and Present on El Salvador, Nicaragua, Honduras, Guatemala, and Costa Rica*. New York: Pantheon Books, 1985.

5. Guzman, Juda. *Memories of a Central American*. New York: Vantage Press, 1988.

Books About the History of the Peace Corps

1. Hoffman, Elizabeth Cobbs. *All You Need is Love: The Peace Corps and the Spirit of the 1960s*. Cambridge, Mass.: Harvard University Press, 2000.

2. Rice, Gerald T. *The Bold Experiment: JFK's Peace Corps*. Notre Dame, Ind.: University of Notre Dame Press, 1985.

3. Stossel, Scott. Sarge: *The Life and Times of Sargent Shriver*. Washington, D.C.: Smithsonian Institution Press, 2004.

4. Meisler, Stanley. *When the World Calls: The Inside Story of the Peace Corps and its First 50 Years*. Boston, Mass.: Beacon Press, 2011.

Books on the Volunteer Experience

1. Dirlam, Sharon. *Beyond Siberia: Two Years in a Forgotten Place*. Santa Barbara, Calif.: McSeas Books, 2004.

2. Casebolt, Marjorie DeMoss. *Margarita: A Guatemalan Peace Corps Experience*. Gig Harbor, Wash.: Red Apple Publishing, 2000.

3. Erdman, Sarah. *Nine Hills to Nambonkaha: Two Years in the Heart of an African Village*. New York, N.Y.: Picador, 2003.

4. Hessler, Peter. *River Town: Two Years on the Yangtze*. New York, N.Y.: Perennial, 2001.

5. Kennedy, Geraldine ed. *From the Center of the Earth: Stories out of the Peace Corps*. Santa Monica, Calif.: Clover Park Press, 1991.

6. Thompsen, Moritz. *Living Poor: A Peace Corps Chronicle*. Seattle, Wash.: University of Washington Press, 1997 (reprint).

Online Spanish Learning Resources

http://www.transparent.com/
Free Spanish short course from Transparent Language.

http://www.byki.com/free_lang_software.pl
Language-learning software based on the flash card system.

http://www.studyspanish.com/
Spanish tutorial provides a good opportunity for self-study; contains lessons, audios, and exercises that are corrected instantly.

http://www.miscositas.com/
Short stories, links, and other exercises for learning Spanish.

LIVING CONDITIONS AND VOLUNTEER LIFESTYLE

Communications

Mail

Letters sent from the United States generally arrive in Honduras in two to three weeks. However, the mail system is not always reliable, and it is not unusual for a letter to take several months to arrive. Packages can take even more time. You will have to pay a tax of approximately 20 to 30 lempiras (about $1-$1.50) at the post office to retrieve any packages.

During pre-service training, mail will be delivered to you at the training site, and your mailing address will be:

"Your Name," PCT
Voluntario del Cuerpo de Paz
Apartado Postal 3158
Tegucigalpa, D.C 11102
Honduras

Volunteers have two options to receive mail: 1) direct delivery to your site via the Honduras postal system; or 2) delivery to the Peace Corps office and the mail can be kept in your mail file at the Peace Corps office.

Option #1: Once you become a Volunteer, you will be responsible for sending your site address to friends and family. We recommend you get a P.O. box (if available at your local post office) if you want to receive correspondence at your site and avoid the cost of coming to the capital city, as well as a delay in delivery time.

Option #2: Mail will be kept in your file at the Peace Corps office until you visit Tegucigalpa for official business. In some instances, Volunteer mail received at the Tegucigalpa office will be forwarded to a Volunteer's site once a month. If Volunteers choose to have their packages mailed to the Peace Corps office, Peace Corps staff will pick up their packages from the Tegucigalpa post office and keep them in the Peace Corps office. Volunteers are responsible for coming to Tegucigalpa to pick them up. All Volunteers must reimburse the Peace Corps for the postal package fee.

We strongly recommend that you establish a regular writing pattern with your friends and relatives, since they might become concerned if they do not hear from you for an extended period of time.

Do not have money or other valuable items sent to you through the mail. Electrical appliances cannot be sent through the mail, as they are prohibited items and could be subject to a custom fine. Letters and packages are sometimes opened by postal workers, and valuable items occasionally disappear. In addition, the process of retrieving a package at the post office can be time consuming, and customs duties may exceed the value of the items sent. If you must have packages sent; we recommend padded envelopes. You will have a bank account at your site, and you can have money wired to that account (but note that the Peace Corps is not allowed to give out your account number). Airline tickets can be paid for in advance and picked up at the airline's office in Tegucigalpa.

Federal Express, UPS, and DHL have offices in Tegucigalpa and can deliver packages to the Peace Corps office. Please do not send any electrical device or appliances via FedEx, UPS, or DHL, as a customs clearance process is required that will cost $90, plus an additional charge of 75 percent of the cost of the device. Please let your family and friends know this before sending any mail. We also encourage you to ask for shipment tracking numbers so you can track packages through the carriers' websites. Remember that these delivery services cannot deliver to a post office box, so you will have to provide the following street address for the Peace Corps office: Colonia Palmira, Avenida República de Chile No. 401, Tegucigalpa 11101 (phone: 504-265-4100).

Please check the Transportation Security Administration (TSA) website for a detailed list of permitted and prohibited items at http://www.tsa.gov/travelers/airtravel/prohibited/permitted-prohibited-items.shtm.

Telephones

International phone service to and from Honduras is relatively good. Hondutel, the telephone agency, has offices in many cities and towns, and some of those offices offer direct lines to U.S. long-distance carriers. You can also call or receive calls from the United States from local phones. To reach you in an emergency, your family can contact the Office of Special Services in Washington, D.C., at (800) 424-8580, ext. 1470 during business hours (Eastern Standard Time) or (301) 790-4749 after hours and on weekends. The Office of Special Services will contact Peace Corps/Honduras immediately and will help you contact your family.

Some Volunteers have telephones in their homes, but most rely on cellphones. Rather than bringing one from the States, purchase it when you get to Honduras. Phone cards are readily available.

Computer, Internet, and Email Access

The Volunteer Resource Center in the Peace Corps office has several computers with Internet access that Volunteers may use for their work. Volunteers may not use Peace Corps staff computers. Regular access to the Volunteer designated computers in the Peace Corps office is not possible during pre-service training because the training site is not near the office. The number of Internet cafes is increasing, especially in major urban centers (including in the town of the training center). Volunteers are encouraged to use the Internet at cafes in or near their communities.

When considering whether or not to bring a laptop or digital camera to Honduras, remember that there is the real possibility of theft or water damage. Counterparts and agencies where you may be assigned to work may not have this type of equipment, or it may be very slow and dated. While it may be beneficial to bring a laptop to augment your personal and professional work, you should consider whether utilization of this technology is sustainable. If you choose to bring a laptop or other valuable equipment, you are strongly encouraged to insure it against theft and damage. You will receive information on personal articles insurance from the Peace Corps prior to departure. Consider Clements International coverage designed for Peace Corps Volunteers. http://www.clements.com/expatriate/peacecorps/personal_property/overview.asp

Housing and Site Location

Volunteer housing varies according to the area of the country and its climate. In much of the southern region, houses are open and airy to provide ventilation. Houses tend to be more enclosed in mountainous areas. Some Volunteers live in houses made of adobe; others live in houses made of wood or cinder blocks or in apartments. Roofing generally consists of clay tiles or corrugated metal. Most Volunteer houses have electricity and running water, though the source of water is often outside the house and water may flow only sporadically. Housing in rural sites may have outdoor latrines instead of indoor plumbing.

Because of the importance of community integration and your personal safety and security, you will be required to live with a host family throughout your two years of service. This is a new, mandatory and nonnegotiable requirement for future Volunteers assigned to Honduras. It is important for you to consider this before accepting the assignment. Living with a host family can be challenging as you adapt to the dynamics of family life, possibly with cramped living conditions, a multigenerational family unit, and limited privacy. However, the benefits are extensive in that it will enhance your safety and security, enable you to more rapidly gain language and cultural skills, and foster your integration into the community. You will be a more active participant in the local community, rather than being viewed as a short-term resident.

During the first six months in your site, you will be required to live within your host family's home, in a separate room that has a locked door. After the first six months and with staff approval, you will have the option of changing host families and moving into a separate building with an enclosed family compound.

Serving in Honduras requires you to make lifestyle adjustments and take precautions to minimize your safety risks. You will need to be aware of your surroundings, be wary of potential crime situations, and exercise good common sense about your personal belongings, where and when you walk, and what transportation you take. You will need to refrain from staying out after dark and returning home late at night. You will need to comply with restrictions placed on travel and transportation within Honduras and other policies that exist to minimize risks to your safety. Sound judgment and professional, mature behavior are required of PC/Honduras Volunteers.

Safe and secure housing is a priority, and Peace Corps/Honduras will help you work with the landlord to make any necessary modifications to improve the safety and security of your home, such as adding deadbolt locks and bars on windows. Additionally, the Peace Corps makes an effort to select sites that offer reasonable and safe transportation. Keep in mind that rural areas of Honduras are more rustic than rural areas of the United States.

Peace Corps Volunteer sites are located throughout Honduras with the exception of the departments of Gracias a Dios and the Bay Islands. The site in which you eventually serve will be selected based upon the local needs of the community, your skills and interests, and the overall goals and objectives of the Peace Corps/Honduras project in which you will work.

Living Allowance and Money Management

As a Volunteer, you will receive a monthly allowance to cover your basic living expenses. The living allowance is reviewed at least once a year through a market survey to ensure that it is adequate for a healthy lifestyle comparable to that of the community in which you live. The allowance is provided in local currency and can range from an equivalency of USD $240 to $320 per month depending on eventual site location. Funds are deposited into your local bank account. You will also receive a housing allowance, which varies according to average housing costs in each region.

The living allowance is intended to cover the cost of food, utilities, household supplies, clothing, recreation and entertainment, transportation, reading materials, and other incidentals. The amount that will be provided to you has been calculated to permit you to live at the modest standards of the people you serve, though you may find that you receive more compensation than your neighbors and even your community partner or supervisor.

You will accrue two days of leave and earn a $24 vacation allowance for each month of service, which is provided in local currency. The vacation allowance is also deposited into your local account each month. Following your swearing in as a Volunteer, you will also receive a one-time settling-in allowance, paid in local currency equivalent to $250, to buy basic household items when you move to your site. This amount is also reviewed annually and adjusted as needed. If the Peace Corps asks you to travel to attend conferences or workshops, you will be given additional funds to cover the related costs of transportation, food, and lodging.

The majority of Volunteers find that they can live comfortably in Honduras with these allowances. While many bring additional money with them for out-of-country travel, the Peace Corps expects Volunteers to live at the same level as their neighbors and colleagues and, therefore, strongly discourages Volunteers from supplementing their income with money brought from home.

Credit cards can be used in the capital and in tourist areas. Traveler's checks can be cashed for a fee.

Food and Diet

Although a wide variety of food is available in Honduras, beans, rice, plantains, and tortillas are the standard fare (*plato tipico*) throughout the country. Medium-size and large communities have markets that sell fruits, vegetables, meat products, milk, cheese, and grains (sometimes including soy and soy products). Volunteers who live in smaller communities, however, may only be able to purchase basic foods such as noodles, canned goods, and rice and may have to travel to nearby markets to purchase perishables.

Vegetarians can maintain a healthy diet in Honduras. However, it may be difficult to maintain a strictly vegetarian diet when you live with host families during pre-service training and the initial two months of service. Families cannot be expected to change their regular diet to meet your needs. These issues will be discussed and explored further during pre-service training.

Transportation

Volunteers in Honduras use public transportation in most situations, even though it can be time-consuming. If you live in a major population center, there will be regular buses from your site to the capital. Smaller communities may have only one bus a day, so you may have to depend on a minivan or truck for transportation. Although in some circumstances it may be necessary to ride in the back of a pickup truck, Volunteers are highly discouraged from traveling this way. Any travel at night is also highly discouraged.

Volunteers are not allowed to drive or ride as a passenger on motorcycles in Honduras. Very rarely are Volunteers permitted to drive a vehicle for work-related activities if their counterpart agency requests them to do so. In this case, the Volunteer must first receive written approval from the country director and then obtain a Honduran driver's license (a valid U.S. driver's license is required to obtain a Honduran license).

In some areas, Volunteers may request a bicycle for work transportation. If approved, the Peace Corps will provide partial funding for the initial purchase. When riding a bicycle, Volunteers are required to wear a helmet, which the Peace Corps will provide and which the Volunteer must return at the close of his or her service. All Volunteers should be prepared to walk regularly, sometimes long distances, to communities within their assignment area. In some cases, because of the distance traveled, Volunteers have to arrange for overnight lodging.

Geography and Climate

For such a small country, Honduras has a wide variety of temperatures—ranging from 60 degrees Fahrenheit to 100 F in the lowlands to 40 F to 90 F in the mountains. In general, the western region is relatively cool, while the southern and eastern regions are moderate to hot in the valleys and colder in the mountains, especially at night. The tropical coasts and large valleys can be very hot and humid. In most parts of Honduras, the rainy season lasts June through November. You should come prepared for all types of climates. The training center is located at a high altitude and gets quite cold in the mornings and evenings, so bring some warm clothes.

Social Activities

Most social activities revolve around family or community events and religious holidays. Hondurans are very hospitable. They often invite Volunteers to their homes for meals and family celebrations, which are a great opportunity to build ties of trust and sharing. You may encounter more traditional gender roles than exist in the United States. While men have freedom of movement, women may be unable to leave their homes unaccompanied after dark. It is not common for women to jog in Honduras, and those who do, never jog alone. In some parts of Honduras, people abuse alcohol, and in other areas, alcohol is prohibited. You need to be moderate and mindful of your own alcohol consumption. A Volunteer whose consumption of alcohol results in behavior that is unsafe, culturally inappropriate or not professional will be disciplined and, depending on the severity of the behavior, may be asked to conclude his or her service early.

Professionalism, Dress, and Behavior

To be effective, Volunteers must be respected by the communities in which they work. The Peace Corps builds its reputation not through massive publicity campaigns, but through its Volunteers, one community at a time. You should be prepared to be a role model throughout your service. When Volunteers find themselves unable to gain and maintain the respect and confidence of their communities, it is almost always due to the Volunteers' failure to meet community standards of behavior. Behavior that is detrimental to the image of the Peace Corps or that threatens the reputation or physical safety of other Volunteers can result in administrative separation from the Peace Corps.

Hondurans are fairly traditional and conservative, especially in smaller villages. During pre-service training, you will learn how to dress and act appropriately in such a society, which has double standards for men and women and often for Hondurans and Americans. Your community is likely to hold you to higher standards because you are a Peace Corps Volunteer.

Dressing appropriately can enhance your credibility, since it reflects your respect for the customs and expectations of the people with whom you live and work. Inappropriate dress, like inappropriate behavior, is something that can set you unnecessarily apart from your community. Until you become well-known by Hondurans, your dress will be an important indicator to them. From the biggest city to the most remote village, you will be judged, especially initially, on your appearance.

You will find that some clothing that is considered appropriate for Hondurans is not considered appropriate for you. As a trainee during pre-service training and as a Volunteer during in-service training events, you are expected to dress as you would on the job. Shirts and shoes must be worn at all times, and shorts and flip-flops are not appropriate.

If you have a tattoo, it is best to keep it covered. Tattoos are often associated with gang affiliation. An anti-gang law allows police to perform searches on people who are considered to be probable gang members. (Though gang tattoos are of a specific nature, you need to be aware of this Honduran reality.)

Hondurans like to dress well and to be neat and clean. Honduran businessmen do not normally wear suits and ties, so male Volunteers can wear a short-sleeved, button-down shirt or nice polo shirt and khakis or nice jeans in professional settings. Casual clothing can be worn at home and in informal situations. Low-cut necklines are not appropriate for women, but sleeveless blouses and dresses are fine, especially in coastal areas and certain valleys. Do not bring any military-style clothing (i.e., olive green or camouflage), which Honduran customs officials reserve the right to confiscate.

These standards indicate appropriate professional dress.

Males
Short sleeve or long sleeve dress shirts
Shirts with collars or polo shirts
Long pants in good condition (jeans, khakis, etc.)
Sneakers or regular shoes with socks

Females
Blouses with collars or polo shirts
Skirts or dresses (not short)
Long pants in good condition (jeans, khakis, etc.)
Mid-calf capri pants
Wearing a bra
Sneakers or regular shoes with socks, sandals

Don't Wear
Shorts of any length
T-shirts
Sleeveless T-shirts or tank tops
Spaghetti strap tops (females)
Mini-skirts (females)
Flip-flops
Earrings (males) —not at any time or any place; (females) no more than two in each ear
Other visible body piercing (including nose and tongue piercings)
Hair length below the bottom of the ear and/or ponytails and/or long untrimmed beards (males)
Camouflage equipment/clothing

Personal Safety

More detailed information about the Peace Corps' approach to safety is contained in the "Health Care and Safety" chapter, but it is an important issue and cannot be overemphasized. As stated in the *Volunteer Handbook,* becoming a Peace Corps Volunteer entails certain safety risks. Living and traveling in an unfamiliar environment (oftentimes alone), having a limited understanding of local language and culture, and being perceived as well-off are some of the factors that can put a Volunteer at risk. Many Volunteers experience varying degrees of unwanted attention and harassment. Petty thefts and burglaries are not uncommon, and incidents of physical and sexual assault do occur, although most Honduras Volunteers complete their two years of service without incident. The Peace Corps has established procedures and policies designed to help you reduce your risks and enhance your safety and security. These procedures and policies, in addition to safety training, will be provided once you arrive in Honduras. Using these tools, you are expected to take responsibility for your safety and well-being.

Each staff member at the Peace Corps is committed to providing Volunteers with the support they need to successfully meet the challenges they will face to have a safe, healthy, and productive service. We encourage Volunteers and families to look at our safety and security information on the Peace Corps website at www.peacecorps.gov/safety.

Information on these pages gives messages on Volunteer health and Volunteer safety. There is a section titled "Safety and Security in Depth." Among topics addressed are the risks of serving as a Volunteer, posts' safety support systems, and emergency planning and communications.

Rewards and Frustrations

You are likely to derive much satisfaction from helping to improve the living conditions of Hondurans and from learning a new culture and language. You will also encounter unusual social and cultural situations that will require flexibility and understanding on your part. By communicating honestly and demonstrating an interest in Honduras and its people, you will soon come to enjoy your community, its customs, and your role as a Volunteer. A low level of interest, motivation, or participation by community members and co-workers, however, may cause you some frustration. You must remember that development takes time and that you may not immediately see any demonstrable impact from your work.

The Peace Corps is not for everyone. Being a Volunteer requires greater dedication and commitment than most other work environments. It is for confident, self-starting, concerned individuals who are interested in participating in the development of other countries and increasing human understanding across cultural barriers. The key to satisfying work as a Peace Corps Volunteer is the ability to establish successful human relationships at all levels with your host family, the community members with whom you work, counterpart agencies and school officials, and your fellow Volunteers. This requires patience, sensitivity, empathy, and a positive, professional attitude. If you have the personal qualities needed to meet the challenges of two years of service in Honduras, you will have a rewarding, enriching, and lasting experience. At the same time, you will contribute to the development of Honduras and leave a part of yourself and your culture behind.

PEACE CORPS TRAINING

Overview of Pre-Service Training

Prior to becoming a Volunteer, you will participate in an 11-week training program in Honduras. Pre-service training incorporates experiential learning and adult learning methodology that is meant to challenge you while preparing you to begin your work as a Volunteer. Pre-service training can be intense, but enjoyable as well.

Upon arrival in Honduras, trainees move in with host families after a brief introductory session. The first three weeks of training takes place in a large group and include trainees from various projects. The fourth through 10th weeks, trainees will move to other communities for field-based training, which focuses on the practical application of project technical skills.

Although you were recruited for a particular project and your training will be tailored to the requirements of that project, all Volunteers are community development facilitators. You will receive theoretical and hands-on training in community analysis, participatory analysis, gender analysis, community development, and integrated community development and become familiar with current development efforts in Honduras. As the weeks pass, you may find you need to adapt both existing skills and new skills to your work environment in Honduras.

Technical Training

Technical training will prepare you to work in Honduras by building on the skills you already have and helping you develop new skills in a manner appropriate to the needs of the country. The Peace Corps staff, Honduras experts, and current Volunteers will conduct the training program. Training places great emphasis on learning how to transfer the skills you have to the community in which you will serve as a Volunteer.

Technical training will include sessions on the general economic and political environment in Honduras and strategies for working within such a framework. You will review your technical sector's goals and will meet with the Honduran agencies and organizations that invited the Peace Corps to assist them. You will be supported and evaluated throughout the training to build the confidence and skills you need to undertake your project activities and be a productive member of your community.

Language Training

As a Peace Corps Volunteer, you will find that language skills are key to personal and professional satisfaction during your service. These skills are critical to your job performance, they help you integrate into your community, and they can ease your personal adaptation to the new surroundings. Therefore, language training is at the heart of the training program. You must successfully meet minimum language requirements to complete training and become a Volunteer. Honduran language instructors teach formal language classes five days a week in small groups of four to five people.

Your language training will incorporate a community-based approach. In addition to classroom time, you will be given assignments to work on outside of the classroom and with your host family. The goal is to get you to a point of basic social communication skills so you can practice and develop language skills further once you are at your site. Prior to being sworn in as a Volunteer, you will work on strategies to continue language studies during your service.

Cross-Cultural Training

As part of your pre-service training, you will live with a Honduran host family. This experience is designed to ease your transition to life at your site. Families go through an orientation conducted by Peace Corps staff to explain the purpose of pre-service training and to assist them in helping you adapt to living in Honduras. Many Volunteers form strong and lasting friendships with their host families.

Cross-cultural and community development training will help you improve your communication skills and understand your role as a facilitator of development. You will be exposed to topics such as community mobilization, conflict resolution, gender and development, nonformal and adult education strategies, and political structures.

As noted above, during pre-service training you will live with two Honduran host families—the first for four weeks during center-based training and a second for six weeks during field-based training. As a member of the family, you will engage in routine family activities and share your time during meals.

Peace Corps/Honduras also requires Volunteers to live the first two months of their service with a host family at their assigned site. The project team will have identified this family prior to your arrival. It is Peace Corps' expectation that your host family will help you connect with your community, serve as additional support with your language learning, assist with your safety and security orientation, and help you assimilate to your new community culture.

Health Training

During pre-service training, you will be given basic medical training and information. You will be expected to practice preventive health care and to take responsibility for your own health by adhering to all medical policies. Trainees are required to attend all medical sessions. The topics include preventive health measures and minor and major medical issues that you might encounter while in Honduras. Nutrition, mental health, setting up a safe living compound, and how to avoid HIV/AIDS and other sexually transmitted diseases (STDs) are also covered.

Safety Training

During the safety training sessions, you will learn how to adopt a lifestyle that reduces your risks at home, at work, and during your travels. You will also learn appropriate, effective strategies for coping with unwanted attention and about your individual responsibility for promoting safety throughout your service.

Additional Trainings During Volunteer Service

In its commitment to institutionalize quality training, the Peace Corps has implemented a training system that provides Volunteers with continual opportunities to examine their commitment to Peace Corps service while increasing their technical and cross-cultural skills. During service, there are usually three training events. The titles and objectives for those trainings are as follows:

- In-service training: *Provides an opportunity for Volunteers to upgrade their technical, language, and project development skills while sharing their experiences and reaffirming their commitment after having served for three to six months.*

- Midterm conference (done in conjunction with technical sector in-service): *Assists Volunteers in reviewing their first year, reassessing their personal and project objectives, and planning for their second year of service.*

- Close of service conference: *Prepares Volunteers for the future after Peace Corps service and reviews their respective projects and personal experiences.*

The number, length, and design of these trainings are adapted to country-specific needs and conditions. The key to the training system is that training events are integrated and interrelated, from the pre-departure orientation through the end of your service, and are planned, implemented, and evaluated cooperatively by the training staff, Peace Corps staff, and Volunteers.

YOUR HEALTH CARE AND
SAFETY IN HONDURAS

The Peace Corps' highest priority is maintaining the good health and safety of every Volunteer. Peace Corps medical programs emphasize the preventive, rather than the curative, approach to disease. The Peace Corps in Honduras maintains a clinic with a full-time medical officer, who takes care of Volunteers' primary health care needs. Additional medical services, such as testing and basic treatment, are also available in Honduras at local hospitals. If you become seriously ill, you will be transported either to an American-standard medical facility in the region or to the United States.

Health Issues in Honduras

Malaria is endemic in almost all of Honduras, so taking anti-malarial medication is mandatory for Volunteers throughout service. Pre-exposure and post-exposure rabies vaccines are also mandatory. Mild to severe viral illnesses like dengue fever (including hemorrhagic dengue) are also threats to health in Honduras.

Existing skin conditions like acne and eczema often worsen in Honduras because of the climate. Sun-aggravated and fungal skin conditions are fairly common. Solar keratosis, a precancerous skin condition, can be acquired from prolonged exposure to the sun without adequate protection.

Helping You Stay Healthy

The Peace Corps will provide you with all the necessary inoculations, medications, and information to stay healthy. Upon your arrival in Honduras, you will receive a medical handbook. At the end of training, you will receive a medical kit with supplies to take care of mild illnesses and first aid needs. The contents of the kit are listed later in this chapter.

During pre-service training, you will have access to basic medical supplies through the medical officer. However, you will be responsible for your own supply of prescription drugs and any other specific medical supplies you require, as the Peace Corps will not order these items during training. Please bring a three-month supply of any prescription drugs you use, since they may not be available here and it may take several months for shipments to arrive.

You will have physicals at midservice and at the end of your service. If you develop a serious medical problem during your service, the medical officer in Honduras will consult with the Office of Medical Services in Washington, D.C. If it is determined that your condition cannot be treated in Honduras, you may be sent out of the country for further evaluation and care.

Multivitamins are not regularly provided since you can easily obtain fruits and vegetables, as well as other nutrients, as part of your daily diet. When a Volunteer shows symptoms caused by a lack of specific vitamins, the medical unit may dispense a vitamin supplement.

Maintaining Your Health

As a Volunteer, you must accept considerable responsibility for your own health. Proper precautions will significantly reduce your risk of serious illness or injury. The adage "An ounce of prevention …" becomes extremely important in areas where diagnostic and treatment facilities are not up to the standards of the United States. The most important of your responsibilities in Honduras is to take the following preventive measures:

Many illnesses that afflict Volunteers worldwide are entirely preventable if proper food and water precautions are taken. These illnesses include food poisoning, parasitic infections, hepatitis A, dysentery, Guinea worms, tapeworms, and typhoid fever. Your medical officer will discuss specific standards for water and food preparation in Honduras during pre-service training.

Honduras has the third highest rate of HIV/AIDS infection in Central America, and the disease is a growing problem. Abstinence is the only certain choice for preventing infection with HIV and other sexually transmitted diseases. You are taking risks if you choose to be sexually active. To lessen risk, use a condom every time you have sex. Whether your partner is a host country citizen, a fellow Volunteer, or anyone else, do not assume this person is free of HIV/AIDS or other STDs. You will receive more information from the medical officer about this important issue.

Volunteers are expected to adhere to an effective means of birth control to prevent an unplanned pregnancy. Your medical officer can help you decide on the most appropriate method to suit your individual needs. Contraceptive methods are available without charge from the medical officer.

It is critical to your health that you promptly report to the medical office or other designated facility for scheduled immunizations, and that you let the medical officer know immediately of significant illnesses and injuries.

Women's Health Information

Pregnancy is treated in the same manner as other Volunteer health conditions that require medical attention but also have programmatic ramifications. The Peace Corps is responsible for determining the medical risk and the availability of appropriate medical care if the Volunteer remains in-country. Given the circumstances under which Volunteers live and work in Peace Corps countries, it is rare that the Peace Corps' medical and programmatic standards for continued service during pregnancy can be met.

If feminine hygiene products are not available for you to purchase on the local market, the Peace Corps medical officer in Honduras will provide them. If you require a specific product, please bring a three-month supply with you.

Due to the nature of Honduras' tropical climate, vaginal yeast infections can occur with greater frequency than usual. Female Volunteers should wear loose-fitting, cotton undergarments to help prevent this condition.

Your Peace Corps Medical Kit

The Peace Corps medical officer will provide you with a kit that contains basic items necessary to prevent and treat illnesses that may occur during service. Kit items can be periodically restocked at the medical office.

Medical Kit Contents

Ace bandages

Adhesive tape

American Red Cross First Aid & Safety Handbook

Antacid tablets (Tums)

Antibiotic ointment (Bacitracin/Neomycin/Polymycin B)

Antiseptic antimicrobial skin cleaner (Hibiclens)

Band-Aids

Butterfly closures

Calamine lotion

Cepacol lozenges

Condoms

Dental floss

Diphenhydramine HCL 25 mg (Benadryl)

Insect repellent stick (Cutter's)

Iodine tablets (for water purification)

Lip balm (Chapstick)

Oral rehydration salts

Oral thermometer (Fahrenheit)

Pseudoephedrine HCL 30 mg (Sudafed)

Robitussin-DM lozenges (for cough)

Scissors

Sterile gauze pads

Tetrahydrozaline eyedrops (Visine)

Tinactin (antifungal cream)

Tweezers

Before You Leave: A Medical Checklist

If there has been any change in your health—physical, mental, or dental—since you submitted your examination reports to the Peace Corps, you must immediately notify the Office of Medical Services. Failure to disclose new illnesses, injuries, allergies, or pregnancy can endanger your health and may jeopardize your eligibility to serve.

If your dental exam was done more than a year ago, or if your physical exam is more than two years old, contact the Office of Medical Services to find out whether you need to update your records. If your dentist or Peace Corps dental consultant has recommended that you undergo dental treatment or repair, you must complete that work and make sure your dentist sends requested confirmation reports or X-rays to the Office of Medical Services.

If you wish to avoid having duplicate vaccinations, contact your physician's office to obtain a copy of your immunization record and bring it to your pre-departure orientation. If you have any immunizations prior to Peace Corps service, the Peace Corps cannot reimburse you for the cost. The Peace Corps will provide all the immunizations necessary for your overseas assignment, either at your pre-departure orientation or shortly after you arrive in Honduras. You do not need to begin taking malaria medication prior to departure.

Bring a three-month supply of any prescription or over-the-counter medication you use on a regular basis, including birth control pills. Although the Peace Corps cannot reimburse you for this three-month supply, it will order refills during your service. While awaiting shipment—which can take several months—you will be dependent on your own medication supply. The Peace Corps will not pay for herbal or nonprescribed medications, such as St. John's wort, glucosamine, selenium, or antioxidant supplements.

You are encouraged to bring copies of medical prescriptions signed by your physician. This is not a requirement, but they might come in handy if you are questioned in transit about carrying a three-month supply of prescription drugs.

If you wear eyeglasses, bring two pairs with you—a pair and a spare. If a pair breaks, the Peace Corps will replace them, using the information your doctor in the United States provided on the eyeglasses form during your examination. The Peace Corps discourages you from using contact lenses during your service to reduce your risk of developing a serious infection or other eye disease. Most Peace Corps countries do not have appropriate water and sanitation to support eye care with the use of contact lenses. The Peace Corps will not supply or replace contact lenses or associated solutions unless an ophthalmologist has recommended their use for a specific medical condition and the Peace Corps' Office of Medical Services has given approval.

If you are eligible for Medicare, are over 50 years of age, or have a health condition that may restrict your future participation in health care plans, you may wish to consult an insurance specialist about unique coverage needs before your departure. The Peace Corps will provide all necessary health care from the time you leave for your pre-departure orientation until you complete your service. When you finish, you will be entitled to the post-service health care benefits described in the Peace Corps *Volunteer Handbook*. You may wish to consider keeping an existing health plan in effect during your service if you think age or pre-existing conditions might prevent you from re-enrolling in your current plan when you return home.

Safety and Security—Our Partnership

Serving as a Volunteer overseas entails certain safety and security risks. Living and traveling in an unfamiliar environment, a limited understanding of the local language and culture, and the perception of being a wealthy American are some of the factors that can put a Volunteer at risk. Property theft and burglaries are not uncommon. Incidents of physical and sexual assault do occur, although almost all Volunteers complete their two years of service without serious personal safety problems.

Beyond knowing that Peace Corps approaches safety and security as a partnership with you, it might be helpful to see how this partnership works. Peace Corps has policies, procedures, and training in place to promote your safety. We depend on you to follow those policies and to put into practice what you have learned. An example of how this works in practice—in this case to help manage the risk of burglary—is:

- Peace Corps assesses the security environment where you will live and work
- Peace Corps inspects the house where you will live according to established security criteria
- Peace Corp provides you with resources to take measures such as installing new locks
- Peace Corps ensures you are welcomed by host country authorities in your new community
- Peace Corps responds to security concerns that you raise
- You lock your doors and windows
- You adopt a lifestyle appropriate to the community where you live
- You get to know neighbors
- You decide if purchasing personal articles insurance is appropriate for you
- You don't change residences before being authorized by Peace Corps
- You communicate concerns that you have to Peace Corps staff

This *Welcome Book* contains sections on: Living Conditions and Volunteer Lifestyle; Peace Corps Training; and Your Health Care and Safety that all include important safety and security information to help you understand this partnership. The Peace Corps makes every effort to give Volunteers the tools they need to function in the safest way possible, because working to maximize the safety and security of Volunteers is our highest priority. Not only do we provide you with training and tools to prepare for the unexpected, but we teach you to identify, reduce, and manage the risks you may encounter.

Factors that Contribute to Volunteer Risk

There are several factors that can heighten a Volunteer's risk, many of which are within the Volunteer's control. By far the most common crime that Volunteers experience is theft. Thefts often occur when Volunteers are away from their sites, in crowded locations (such as markets or on public transportation), and when leaving items unattended.

Before you depart for Honduras there are several measures you can take to reduce your risk:

o   Leave valuable objects in U.S.

o   Leave copies of important documents and account numbers with someone you trust in the U.S.

o   Purchase a hidden money pouch or *"dummy"* wallet as a decoy

o   Purchase personal articles insurance

After you arrive in Honduras, you will receive more detailed information about common crimes, factors that contribute to Volunteer risk, and local strategies to reduce that risk. For example, Volunteers in Honduras learn to:

o   Choose safe routes and times for travel, and travel with someone trusted by the community whenever possible

o   Make sure one's personal appearance is respectful of local customs

o   Avoid high-crime areas

o   Know the local language to get help in an emergency

o   Make friends with local people who are respected in the community

o   Limit alcohol consumption

As you can see from this list, you must be willing to work hard and adapt your lifestyle to minimize the potential for being a target for crime. As with anywhere in the world, crime does exist in Honduras. You can reduce your risk by avoiding situations that place you at risk and by taking precautions. Crime at the village or town level is less frequent than in the large cities; people know each other and generally are less likely to steal from their neighbors. Tourist attractions in large towns are favorite worksites for pickpockets.

The following are other security concerns in Honduras of which you should be aware:

There is increased gang activity in all the major cities in Honduras, and gangs have begun to make inroads into rural areas as well. Assaults and robberies attributed to gangs have been reported on buses, so Volunteers are prohibited from traveling on certain bus routes. In addition, Volunteers are encouraged to limit their nighttime activities, which may require a modification in social habits.

Volunteers have been held up at gun and knife point. Theft on the streets of bags, cellphones, and money is not uncommon. Some Volunteers have had their wallets and backpacks (including laptops, electronics) taken while riding on buses.

Recent economic developments have increased criminal activity in all areas of the country. Kidnappings of national and foreign citizens have occurred, and drive-by motorcyclists in the capital sometimes snatch people's purses or bags without stopping. Being alone in an isolated area increases the risk of criminal activity.

Some areas of Honduras are banned or highly discouraged for Volunteers. The banned areas include all beaches at night, much of San Pedro Sula, the road/area from San Pedro Sula north to Puerto Cortes and then westward to the border with Guatemala, and some areas of Olancho. Peace Corps/Honduras expects Volunteers to comply at all times with its safety and security regulations. Volunteers must take responsibility for their actions and make the best choices possible to keep themselves safe.

While whistles and exclamations may be fairly common on the street, this behavior can be reduced if you dress conservatively, abide by local cultural norms, and respond according to the training you will receive.

Staying Safe: Don't Be a Target for Crime

You must be prepared to take on a large degree of responsibility for your own safety. You can make yourself less of a target, ensure that your home is secure, and develop relationships in your community that will make you an unlikely victim of crime. While the factors that contribute to your risk in Honduras may be different, in many ways you can do what you would do if you moved to a new city anywhere: Be cautious, check things out, ask questions, learn about your neighborhood, know where the more risky locations are, use common sense, and be aware. You can reduce your vulnerability to crime by integrating into your community, learning the local language, acting responsibly, and abiding by Peace Corps policies and procedures. Serving safely and effectively in Honduras will require that you accept some restrictions on your current lifestyle.

Strategies to reduce the risk/impact of theft:

- Know the environment and choose safe routes/times for travel
- Avoid high-crime areas per Peace Corps guidance
- Know the vocabulary to get help in an emergency
- Carry valuables in different pockets/places
- Carry a "dummy" wallet as a decoy

Strategies to reduce the risk/impact of burglary:

- Live with a local family or on a family compound
- Put strong locks on doors and keep valuables in a lock box or trunk
- Leave irreplaceable objects at home in the U.S.
- Purchase the Peace Corps-recommended personal property insurance
- Follow Peace Corps guidelines on maintaining home security

Strategies to reduce the risk/impact of assault:

- Make friends with local people who are respected in the community
- Make sure your appearance is respectful of local customs; don't draw negative attention to yourself by wearing inappropriate clothing
- Get to know local officials, police, and neighbors
- Travel with someone trusted in your community whenever possible
- Avoid known high crime areas
- Limit alcohol consumption

Support from Staff

If a trainee or Volunteer is the victim of a safety incident, Peace Corps staff is prepared to provide support. All Peace Corps posts have procedures in place to respond to incidents of crime committed against Volunteers. The first priority for all posts in the aftermath of an incident is to ensure the Volunteer is safe and receiving medical treatment as needed. After assuring the safety of the Volunteer, Peace Corps staff response may include reassessing the Volunteer's worksite and housing arrangements and making any adjustments, as needed. In some cases, the nature of the incident may necessitate a site or housing transfer. Peace Corps staff will also assist Volunteers with preserving their rights to pursue legal sanctions against the perpetrators of the crime. It is very important that Volunteers report incidents as they occur, not only to protect their peer Volunteers, but also to preserve the future right to prosecute. Should Volunteers decide later in the process that they want to proceed with the prosecution of their assailant, this option may no longer exist if the evidence of the event has not been preserved at the time of the incident.

Crime Data for Honduras

The country-specific data chart below shows the average annual rates of the major types of crimes reported by Peace Corps Volunteers/trainees in Honduras compared to all other Region programs as a whole. It can be understood as an approximation of the number of reported incidents per 100 Volunteers in a year.

The incidence rate for each type of crime is the number of crime events relative to the Volunteer/trainee population. It is expressed on the chart as a ratio of crime to Volunteer and trainee years (or V/T years, which is a measure of 12 full months of V/T service) to allow for a statistically valid way to compare crime data across countries.

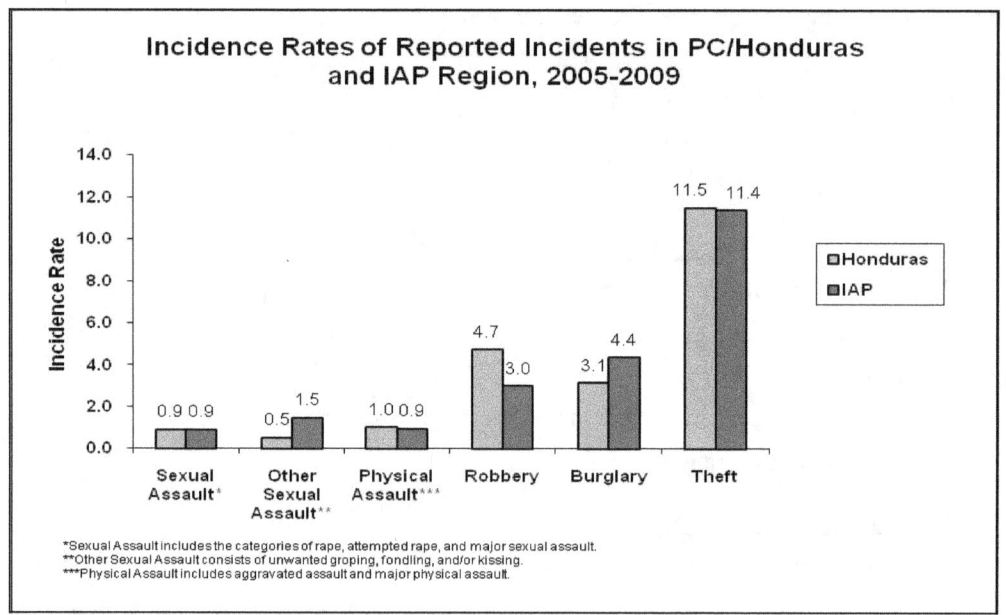

Few Peace Corps Volunteers are victims of serious crimes and crimes that do occur overseas are investigated and prosecuted by local authorities through the local courts system. If you are the victim of a crime, you will decide if you wish to pursue prosecution. If you decide to prosecute, Peace Corps will be there to assist you. One of our tasks is to ensure you are fully informed of your options and understand how the local legal process works. Peace Corps will help you ensure your rights are protected to the fullest extent possible under the laws of the country.

If you are the victim of a serious crime, you will learn how to get to a safe location as quickly as possible and contact your Peace Corps office. It's important that you notify Peace Corps as soon as you can so Peace Corps can provide you with the help you need.

Volunteer Safety Support in Honduras

The Peace Corps' approach to safety is a five-pronged plan to help you stay safe during your service and includes the following: information sharing, Volunteer training, site selection criteria, a detailed emergency action plan, and protocols for addressing safety and security incidents. Honduras' in-country safety program is outlined below.

The Peace Corps/Honduras office will keep you informed of any issues that may impact Volunteer safety through information sharing. Regular updates will be provided in Volunteer newsletters and in memorandums from the country director. In the event of a critical situation or emergency, you will be contacted through the emergency communication network. An important component of the capacity of Peace Corps to keep you informed is your buy-in to the partnership concept with the Peace Corps staff. It is expected that you will do your part in ensuring that Peace Corps staff members are kept apprised of your movements in-country so they are able to inform you.

Volunteer training will include sessions on specific safety and security issues in Honduras. This training will prepare you to adopt a culturally appropriate lifestyle and exercise judgment that promotes safety and reduces risk in your home, at work, and while traveling. Safety training is offered throughout service and is integrated into the language, cross-cultural aspects, health, and other components of training. You will be expected to successfully complete all training competencies in a variety of areas, including safety and security, as a condition of service.

Certain **site selection criteria** are used to determine safe housing for Volunteers before their arrival. The Peace Corps staff works closely with host communities and counterpart agencies to help prepare them for a Volunteer's arrival and to establish expectations of their respective roles in supporting the Volunteer. Each site is inspected before the Volunteer's arrival to ensure placement in appropriate, safe, and secure housing and worksites. Site selection is based, in part, on any relevant site history; access to medical, banking, postal, and other essential services; availability of communications, transportation, and markets; different housing options and living arrangements; and other Volunteer support needs.

You will also learn about Peace Corps/Honduras' **detailed emergency action plan,** which is implemented in the event of civil or political unrest or a natural disaster. When you arrive at your site, you will complete and submit a site locator form with your address, contact information, and a map to your house. If there is a security threat, you will gather with other Volunteers in Honduras at predetermined locations until the situation is resolved or the Peace Corps decides to evacuate.

Finally, in order for the Peace Corps to be fully responsive to the needs of Volunteers, it is imperative that Volunteers immediately report any security incident to the Peace Corps office. The Peace Corps has established **protocols for addressing safety and security incidents** in a timely and appropriate manner, and it collects and evaluates safety and security data to track trends and develop strategies to minimize risks to future Volunteers.

DIVERSITY AND CROSS-CULTURAL ISSUES

In fulfilling its mandate to share the face of America with host countries, the Peace Corps is making special efforts to assure that all of America's richness is reflected in the Volunteer corps. More Americans of color are serving in today's Peace Corps than at any time in recent history. Differences in race, ethnic background, age, religion, and sexual orientation are expected and welcomed among our Volunteers. Part of the Peace Corps' mission is to help dispel any notion that Americans are all of one origin or race and to establish that each of us is as thoroughly American as the other despite our many differences.

Our diversity helps us accomplish that goal. In other ways, however, it poses challenges. In Honduras, as in other Peace Corps host countries, Volunteers' behavior, lifestyle, background, and beliefs are judged in a cultural context very different from their own. Certain personal perspectives or characteristics commonly accepted in the United States may be quite uncommon, unacceptable, or even repressed in Honduras.

Outside of Honduras' capital, residents of rural communities have had relatively little direct exposure to other cultures, races, religions, and lifestyles. What people view as typical American behavior or norms may be a misconception, such as the belief that all Americans are rich and have blond hair and blue eyes. The people of Honduras are justly known for their generous hospitality to foreigners; however, members of the community in which you will live may display a range of reactions to cultural differences that you present.

To ease the transition and adapt to life in Honduras, you may need to make some temporary, yet fundamental compromises in how you present yourself as an American and as an individual. For example, female trainees and Volunteers may not be able to exercise the independence available to them in the United States; political discussions need to be handled with great care; and some of your personal beliefs may best remain undisclosed. You will need to develop techniques and personal strategies for coping with these and other limitations. The Peace Corps staff will lead diversity and sensitivity discussions during pre-service training and will be on call to provide support, but the challenge ultimately will be your own.

Overview of Diversity in Honduras

The Peace Corps staff in Honduras recognizes the adjustment issues that come with diversity and will endeavor to provide support and guidance. During pre-service training, several sessions will be held to discuss diversity and coping mechanisms. We look forward to having male and female Volunteers from a variety of races, ethnic groups, ages, religions, and sexual orientations, and hope that you will become part of a diverse group of Americans who take pride in supporting one another and demonstrating the richness of American culture. One aspect of cultural adaptation is being sensitive to the diversity among the Volunteer population.

In addition to the support provided to Volunteers by Peace Corps/Honduras staff, several peer support groups exist to help Volunteers serve effectively. COLORS is an organization of Volunteers whose vision is to create an environment where diversity is respected and celebrated in fulfillment of the Peace Corps' goal of intercultural exchange. The Gay, Lesbian, or Bisexual Experience (GLOBE) was formed in 1998 to promote the health and well-being of gay, lesbian, and bisexual Volunteers by providing direct support and by educating the Peace Corps community. Volunteers Offering Support (VOS) is a peer network and is available to any Volunteer or trainee who needs a supportive network of concerned Volunteers trained in active listening. VOS members are strategically located throughout Honduras and can be contacted via email or cellphone. MARV (Married Volunteers) provides married Volunteer couples with a group whose purpose is social support and education as to the opportunities and challenges of married Volunteers. REF (Religious Equality Forum) is a new group for all religious/spiritual Volunteers to share experiences and diverse backgrounds in a proselytizing-free environment. Lastly, OAKS (Older and Knowing Souls) is a support group for the needs of older Volunteers in Honduras.

What Might a Volunteer Face?

Possible Issues for Female Volunteers

You should be prepared for unwanted attention from Honduran men simply because you are an American woman. American women are sometimes perceived as being "easy" because of stereotypes portrayed on American TV shows and movies aired on Honduran television. It is very common to receive stares, comments, or requests for dates or sex on the street and in other situations. In addition, women often are not taken as seriously as men in their jobs and may not receive the respect that is readily given to both American and Honduran men. In Honduran culture, a woman is viewed as either a "mother" or a "daughter." If you are not married, you may be treated like a daughter or a child instead of a grown woman.

Honduran women have very specific, traditional roles (e.g., they generally do not work outside of the home), which some Hondurans may think female Volunteers should adopt. Working with men can be difficult if they refuse to believe a woman is capable of work other than cleaning the house or raising children. Working with women can be difficult when they cannot understand why a woman would want to do anything that is not "women's work." Honduran men also have specific roles, and machismo, or manliness, is considered very important. Men are expected to be dominant in almost all aspects of society; they are expected to smoke, drink, pursue women, be strong, and be willing to discipline their wife and children. Thus, male Volunteers who do not drink, smoke, or like to pursue women openly may be chided for not being manly enough. Both female and male Volunteers will learn strategies to handle these situations during pre-service training.

Volunteer Comments

"When I found out I was coming to Honduras, people told me I should dye my hair from blond to brown so I would get less unwanted attention. I quickly found this would have been a silly thing to do. As a foreigner, you will get attention whether you want it or not, whether you dye your hair or wear really conservative clothes. It is better to just be yourself, because you will find that most of the time, people are respectful and as they get to know you, they will not treat you in an inappropriate way. There will always be comments and attention that bothers you, but your friends and co-workers you meet in the community will counterbalance this with the kind of attention, relationships, and interchange that really makes the Peace Corps experience special. You will also find, if you stand up for yourself when needed and remind people that you live here and don't appreciate the catcalls, they will start to change as well."

"Machismo is a fact of life in Honduras. It affects work, relationships, even a simple trip to the market. Every woman has her own way of dealing with unwanted attention, but regardless, on some level it always bothers you, makes you feel a little smaller. It's important to remind yourself that a *piropois* is literally a compliment, and Honduran women generally take them as such. Still, it can be one of the most difficult things for female Volunteers to cope with. Machismo can also affect women's efficacy in the workplace where, regardless of credentials, women are often not taken as seriously as men and are still expected to be submissive. Female Volunteers have to work extra hard to maintain professional relationships with male co-workers, and set boundaries regarding personal interaction. It makes it difficult to have male friends as well, because in Honduras men and women are generally not 'just friends.' Often, female Volunteers are inspired by their difficulties to be advocates for change in gender roles in their communities, working with women's groups and young girls to build self-esteem and give them the tools to overcome machismo and traditional gender expectations and be self-sufficient and independent."

Possible Issues for Volunteers of Color

African-American Volunteers may be viewed as less professionally competent than white Volunteers. They may be called *negrita*, *trigueña*, or other words that distinguish them as dark-skinned. Although these terms are not necessarily derogatory, Volunteers may initially feel demeaned by them. In addition, Hondurans may not believe you are an American, thinking you must come from the north coast of Honduras or the Bay Islands, which have a heavy concentration of Garifuna or black Caribs.

Hondurans may expect Hispanic Americans to interact socially with more ease. Likewise, Volunteers with Latino surnames may be expected to speak Spanish fluently and may not be perceived as being North American.

Asian Americans, too, are often identified more by their cultural heritage than by their American citizenship. Hondurans may expect you to be a kung fu expert because of stereotypes based on behavior observed in films. Many Asians are labeled as Chinese, regardless of their actual ethnic background. Honduras' current or historical involvement with certain Asian countries, or the presence of Asian merchants in the community, may also have an impact on how Asian-American Volunteers are perceived.

If you would like more information on the COLORS Peace Corps Volunteer group in Honduras, please visit its Yahoo group home page at: http://groups.yahoo.com/group/PchCOLORS. For specific questions, please email the group at: PchCOLORS@yahoogroups.com.

Volunteer Comments

"Being an African-American Volunteer in Honduras had been a wonderful experience. Interestingly enough, my ethnicity was never really as apparent during my time as a Peace Corps Volunteer as much as it was during the first days of training. Being the only African American in my training group was a bit isolating initially, but once I got to know my fellow *Aspirantes*, there was a bond between us and they served as a great source of support.

"The biggest advantage has been that initially I am usually mistaken for a Honduran Garifuna; Afro-Caribs that live primarily on the north coast and the Bay Islands. This has worked really well for my site on the north coast because I am accepted into the community more readily and treated as a fellow local rather than a *gringa* (a Western foreigner). One woman put it best when she said to her friend about me, *"Ella es como nosotros"* (She is like us). Just like that, without having to prove myself, I was accepted into the community! I was able to gain *confianza* (trust) almost instantaneously, unlike my fellow PCVs, who have to work for months to gain that kind of trust with their communities.

"Being perceived as a Garifuna also has some disadvantages, namely the implicit expectation that I am a native Spanish speaker. Although, once they realize that you are not Honduran, not only are they always willing to help you with your Spanish, they are also making arrangements for you to spend time with their family and teach you Garifuna, their indigenous language. This can be a great way to spend your down time.

"Also, among Garifuna Hondurans, there is an expectation that you are like family and expectations are placed on you, like there would be in any family. This can be really challenging to balance your time and resources. Initially you might feel obligated to go to every function and outing, but with time, you will learn how to balance your time and resources to make it work best for you.

"My service in Honduras has been challenging at times, but overall, it was a great experience that I believed was enriched because I am African-American. There are challenges to be sure—little things like "What do I do with my hair?" to larger concerns such as, "How a can I make a lasting positive impact on this community?" Ultimately, the immediate acceptance that came with being viewed as a native child, although nevertheless being a foreigner, allowed me to experience many wonderful opportunities of cultural exchange and bonding that made my service all the more gratifying."

Possible Issues for Senior Volunteers

Senior Volunteers often receive more respect from Hondurans than younger Volunteers do, but they need to be aware of possible issues of inclusion and acceptance by fellow Volunteers. Others in the Peace Corps community may have little understanding of the lives and experiences of seniors, and seniors may not receive the personal support they desire from younger Volunteers. Older Volunteers may not feel comfortable sharing personal, sexual, or health concerns with younger members of the Peace Corps staff. On the other hand, seniors may find that younger Volunteers look to them for advice and support. While some seniors find this a very enjoyable part of their experience, others choose not to fill this role.

Older trainees sometimes encounter a lack of attention to their particular needs for an effective learning environment and may need to be assertive in developing an individual approach to language learning, for instance. Senior Volunteers should consider designating a Power of Attorney for management of their financial affairs during service.

Volunteer Comments

"In my site I am commonly referred to as '*Doña Barbara.*' The fact that I have been married and am a mother and a grandmother is an experience I share with local people, especially women. Banks and other establishments have special, shorter lines for people over 60 (*tercera edád*). People often give me their seat on the bus. I have a number of Honduran friends of all ages. On the other hand, I am occasionally treated in a patronizing way or called grandmother (*abuelita*) or little mother (*mamacita*) or even (rarely) little old lady (*viejita*). Some kids make fun of me or point when I ride by on my bike with a bicycle helmet—'Doña Barbara is riding a bike. Look! Look!' Nor am I totally exempt, at age 63, from marriage proposals from younger men looking for a ticket to the United States. Sometimes younger Volunteers are assumed to be my children. Because of my age and the general respect I command in my town, I feel it especially important that I dress conservatively, act properly, and observe local customs."

"Although I tend to agree with the issues that senior Volunteers may have to contend with, so far they have not been problematic for me. Fellow trainees and staff have been very friendly and inclusive. It has been easy to share my experiences and discuss concerns with them. I have stayed in hotel rooms, been to restaurants and movies with other trainees and have not been uncomfortable. Although my social and recreational interests sometimes differ from theirs, I am interested in hearing about what they like to do and talk about. It's refreshing. While it's probably true that those of us who are older have less need for contact with others, I agree that it is a good idea to seek out other older Volunteers. I have talked with several of them about possibly getting together for a weekend or a vacation trip. I 'feel my age' when walking a long way uphill with a heavy pack, but I manage to make it. And I've been able to do my fair share of work in agriculture projects. Learning Spanish is difficult, but I try hard and everyone is helpful. Respect is important, and I feel I've given it as well as received it in Honduras. I hope the Peace Corps will continue to support diversity."

Possible Issues for Gay, Lesbian, or Bisexual Volunteers

Homosexuality is not illegal in Honduras; however, it is met with varying degrees of acceptance by Hondurans, one's community, and other Volunteers. Volunteers generally choose not to be open about their sexual orientation in their communities, but often do reveal it to individuals with whom they have built a trusting relationship. You will have to decide for yourself how open to be.

Like most Volunteers, you may have difficulties with the *machismo* in Honduras. Lesbian and bisexual women should be prepared to field questions regarding boyfriends, marriage, and sex. Likewise, gay and bisexual men will be asked about girlfriends and may find themselves in situations in which men brag about sexual conquests or objectify women. You will have to develop personal strategies to deal with such situations.

Peace Corps staff members are committed to supporting gay and bisexual Volunteers, but they may not always know how best to do so. You will need to be patient and willing to educate staff and other Volunteers about your needs. Peace Corps/Honduras has a Volunteer support group called GLOBE (for Gay, Lesbian, or Bisexual Experience) that meets at least twice a year and maintains an email address. If you would like to contact GLOBE before your departure, send an email to globehonduras@yahoogroups.com.

Volunteer Comments:

"My experience as a gay Volunteer has been positive within the Peace Corps community (i.e. administration, staff, and Volunteers), and I have had the utmost support from peers in my training group. In my village, I decided to closet myself because of ignorant beliefs about homosexuality. However, this decision didn't stop me from successfully completing my projects. I have formed some amazing friendships in my village, and I cherish the wonderful memories. Though it has been hard to be back in the closet, I've been able to teach Hondurans to treat others for who they are and not what they are."

"One of the first things that occurred to me during training was how seemingly conservative and straight my training group peers were. As an openly bisexual woman, I suddenly realized just how important the half-gay part of myself was to me. It had never occurred to me that I might have to close the closet door completely to everyone I met over the next two years. Once at my site, I quickly realized that within the Honduran community, I could easily mask my sexual orientation without harm to the rest of my identity. I am often asked about boyfriends—why I don't have any and whether I want to marry a Honduran man. I got involved with GLOBE, the gay, lesbian, and bisexual support group, and connected with my not-so-straight Peace Corps peers. This gave me the sense of community that I was lacking and allowed me to be myself, with no questions asked."

"Being a gay Volunteer in Honduras has presented many different challenges but also opportunities. The major challenge I faced during my service was being in the closet to my community after years of being openly gay. Often I felt that closeting myself was a barrier to developing a trusting relationship with my community. Although I have, for the most part, remained closeted to my community, I have formed friendships where I felt comfortable to come out. This has presented opportunities to discuss different ideas about homosexuality and being gay in the United States versus Honduras and whether or not I come away from a discussion agreeing on certain issues, I always feel I have a better understanding of the culture."

Possible Religious Issues for Volunteers

Honduras is a Christian country, with the Roman Catholic and Evangelical Christian faiths being predominant. There is little knowledge among Hondurans of other world religions, and Volunteers of other faiths may experience stereotyping or misinformation about their religion. Volunteers should be prepared to be challenged by local people when they express or practice their own beliefs, but this is primarily the result of curiosity or ignorance. Many Volunteers choose not to draw attention to their own religion to avoid awkward or sensitive situations. This is a very personal choice that can only be made on an individual basis. There is a strong Jewish community in Tegucigalpa and San Pedro Sula that has been very welcoming to Jewish Volunteers. Those who want more information about religious challenges in Honduras are encouraged to contact the REF support group.

Volunteer Comments

"When I first arrived in Honduras I was extremely hesitant to share that I was Jewish due to tales of anti-Semitism I had heard on more than one occasion. However, I learned that there is no organized anti-Semitic movement in Honduras, but there is widespread ignorance, as most people have never even met a Jew. Most Hondurans' knowledge about the Jewish faith comes from what they have read in the Bible. Most people will show interest instead of disdain, and there is never any danger involved. When all is said and done, it is up to the individual if he or she chooses to share with other people, but it can be one of the greatest exchanges of culture that you have during your stay in Honduras. During my service here I have had Shabbat dinner with Honduran friends, and I have had long discussions on cultural differences and similarities. For me, it has been more of a bonding experience than a deterrent."

"As a Peace Corps Volunteer, I have not practiced Judaism like I did in the States. I knew that about 200 Jews live in Honduras and that there are two synagogues, but I wasn't sure how average people would react to learning that I practiced a distinctly different religion. I learned that it was better to avoid the subject, especially since I spoke very little Spanish. Rather than go into the differences between Judaism and Christianity, it was better to say that I practiced a religion very few people here practiced, but that I believed in God. I decided to avoid explaining anything in depth to minimize my differences from others. At the same time, I conscientiously explained to other Volunteers and staff why I do some things differently. While I wasn't able to attend services at the synagogue with regularity, I made a point of seeking out other Jewish Volunteers or members of the Jewish community to celebrate the High Holy Days, Hanukkah, and Passover. Over time I began to feel comfortable with certain members of my town and began to explain what it is to be a Jew. I made a point of sharing traditional foods with my Honduran friends, including bagels, challah, and falafel. For the most part, I received a good response. For virtually everyone, I was the first Jew they had ever met. One last thing: Many people here don't realize that mortadella, hot dogs, sausage, and ham contain pork!"

Possible Issues for Volunteers With Disabilities

There is little consciousness of the needs of the physically challenged in Honduras. Volunteers with physical disabilities may find mobility difficult because the infrastructure does not make many accommodations for disabled people. Nevertheless, as part of the medical clearance process, the Peace Corps Office of Medical Services determined that you were physically and emotionally capable, with or without reasonable accommodations, to perform a full tour of Volunteer service in Honduras without unreasonable risk of harm to yourself or interruption of your service. The Peace Corps/Honduras staff will work with disabled Volunteers to make reasonable accommodations in training, housing, jobsites, and other areas to enable them to serve safely and effectively.

Possible Issues for Married Volunteers

Being a married couple in the Peace Corps has its advantages and its challenges. It helps to have someone by your side to share your experience with, but there are also cultural expectations that can cause stress in a marriage. It is important to remember that you are in a foreign country with new rules and you need to be open-minded about cultural differences. A couple may have to take on some new roles. A married man may be encouraged by Hondurans to be the more dominant member in the relationship, be encouraged to make decisions independently of his spouse, or be ridiculed when he performs domestic tasks. A married woman may find herself in a less independent role than she is accustomed to or may be expected to perform "traditional" domestic chores such as cooking or cleaning. Other issues may also arise: One spouse may be more enthusiastic about Peace Corps service, be better able to adapt to the new environment, or be less homesick than the other. Competition may arise if one spouse learns the language or other skills faster than the other. Though most couples in Peace Corps/Honduras have served together successfully, there have been couples who have split during service. Sometimes the couple returns to the States and other times, one spouse has departed while the other spouse has remained. It is important that couples discuss frankly and honestly their preparedness to address the challenges they will experience. Peace Corps/Honduras' married Volunteer support group, MARV, should be helpful in this process.

Volunteer Comments

"Serving as a married couple in the Peace Corps has been both a rewarding and a challenging experience. It has strengthened our relationship in many ways because we have had to deal with situations that when living and working in the U.S., we never encountered. As a married Volunteer, you have the advantage of always having someone to talk to and with whom to share successes and failures. Upon finishing your two years with the Peace Corps, you get to return to the States with someone who has shared this once-in-a-lifetime experience with you and can help you readjust to life in the States while not forgetting the great memories you have of your time in Honduras.

"One of the difficulties of being married in the Peace Corps is that depending on the level of language you come with, married Volunteers may struggle more with language learning due to the fact that much of your time is spent together. When you're already living with your best friend, loneliness is less likely encountered and, therefore, married Volunteers may not feel as 'pushed' as a single Volunteer to get out there and make friends with people in their community.

"You will go through ups and downs during your service like all Volunteers. As a couple, you won't always be feeling the same way about your service at any given time so it is important to learn how to support your spouse when he or she is feeling down and also when he/she is enjoying his/her work and life here in Honduras (even when you're not)."

Another couple writes:

"As married Volunteers, we have distinct rewards and challenges compared to our single Volunteer friends. Some of these rewards include companionship, love, and support during some of the more difficult times of Peace Corps service. We also have the benefits of sharing a household and expenses on a modest living allowance. We are building wonderful memories as a couple and growing with each other as we learn life lessons and experience new things together.

"However, being married in the Peace Corps also has its difficulties. Married Volunteers spend a lot of time together, especially in our particular case because my husband and I share the same counterpart and work on many projects together. This could end up being a lot more time than you ever spent together in the States and will take time to adjust to.

"The challenges and frustrations we all deal with as Peace Corps Volunteers can sometimes add stress to a marriage. Then, of course, there is the Honduran perspective on marriage, and the trials and tribulations we face when our relationship does not fit their mold of what a marriage should entail. Finally, married Volunteers might encounter a little bit of resentment from other single Volunteers because of the unique benefits married Volunteers have.

"However, I feel being married has its benefits no matter where one is, at home or in the Peace Corps. If a couple's relationship can withstand the stress and challenges of service, your relationship will benefit and your bond will grow stronger from your time here together. It is a wonderful opportunity to experience the world through the lens of another culture and to share those experiences with your spouse. Your time as married Volunteers in Honduras is an opportunity to develop a unique perspective together on the world and on life itself.

"You will have a lot more time together as a couple than you were probably used to in the States and this can take some getting used to. Be sure to find 'me,' time but also find time to do fun things together as a couple. With fewer 'entertainment' options than in the States, it's important to find something that you can enjoy together, however simple it may be–cooking, traveling, getting a pet, gardening, board games, etc."

FREQUENTLY ASKED QUESTIONS

How much luggage am I allowed to bring to Honduras?

Most airlines have baggage size and weight limits and assess charges for transport of baggage that exceeds those limits. The Peace Corps has its own size and weight limits and will not pay the cost of transport for baggage that exceeds these limits. The Peace Corps' allowance is two checked pieces of luggage with combined dimensions of both pieces not to exceed 107 inches (length + width + height) and a carry-on bag with dimensions of no more than 45 inches. Checked baggage should not exceed 80 pounds total with a maximum weight of 50 pounds for any one bag.

Peace Corps Volunteers are not allowed to take pets, weapons, explosives, radio transmitters (shortwave radios are permitted), automobiles, or motorcycles to their overseas assignments. Do not pack flammable materials or liquids such as lighter fluid, cleaning solvents, hair spray, or aerosol containers. This is an important safety precaution. Please check the Transportation Security Administration (TSA) website for a detailed list of permitted and prohibited items at http://www.tsa.gov/travelers/airtravel/prohibited/permitted-prohibited-items.shtm.

What is the electric current in Honduras?

Both 110 volts, 60 cycles (the U.S. standard), and 220 volts can be found in houses in Honduras. The outlets often are close to each other and easily confused, so you need to know which outlet to use. Some Volunteers do not have electricity in their houses or have it only for a few hours a day.

How much money should I bring?

Volunteers are expected to live at the same level as the people in their community. You will be given a settling-in allowance and a monthly living allowance, which should cover your expenses. Volunteers often wish to bring additional money for vacation travel to other countries. Credit cards and traveler's checks are preferable to cash. If you choose to bring extra money, bring the amount that will suit your own travel plans and needs.

When can I take vacation and have people visit me?

Each Volunteer accrues two vacation days per month of service (excluding training). Leave may not be taken during training, the first three months of service, or the last three months of service, except in conjunction with an authorized emergency leave. Family and friends are welcome to visit you after pre-service training and the first three months of service as long as their stay does not interfere with your work. Extended stays at your site are not encouraged and may require permission from your country director. The Peace Corps is not able to provide your visitors with visa, medical, or travel assistance.

Will my belongings be covered by insurance?

The Peace Corps does not provide insurance coverage for personal effects; Volunteers are ultimately responsible for the safekeeping of their personal belongings. However, you can purchase personal property insurance before you leave. If you wish, you may contact your own insurance company; additionally, insurance application forms will be provided, and we encourage you to consider them carefully. Volunteers should not ship or take valuable items overseas. Jewelry, watches, radios, cameras, and expensive appliances are subject to loss, theft, and breakage, and in many places, satisfactory maintenance and repair services are not available.

Do I need an international driver's license?

Volunteers in Honduras do not need an international driver's license because they are prohibited from operating privately owned motorized vehicles. Most urban travel is by bus or taxi. Rural travel ranges from buses and minibuses to trucks, bicycles, and lots of walking. On very rare occasions, a Volunteer may be asked to drive a sponsor's vehicle, but this can occur only with prior written permission from the country director. Should this occur, the Volunteer may obtain a local driver's license. A U.S. driver's license will facilitate the process, so bring it with you just in case.

What should I bring as gifts for Honduran friends and my host family?

This is not a requirement. A token of friendship is sufficient. Some gift suggestions include knickknacks for the house; pictures, books, or calendars of American scenes; souvenirs from your area; hard candies that will not melt or spoil; or photos to give away.

Where will my site assignment be when I finish training and how isolated will I be?

Peace Corps trainees are not assigned to individual sites until after they have completed pre-service training. This gives Peace Corps staff the opportunity to assess each trainee's technical and language skills prior to assigning sites, in addition to finalizing site selections with their ministry counterparts. If feasible, you may have the opportunity to provide input on your site preferences, including geographical location, distance from other Volunteers, and living conditions. However, keep in mind that many factors influence the site selection process and that the Peace Corps cannot guarantee placement where you would ideally like to be. Most Volunteers live in small towns or in rural villages and are usually within one hour from another Volunteer. Some sites require a 10- to 12-hour drive from the capital. There is at least one Volunteer based in each of the regional capitals and about five to eight Volunteers in the capital city.

How can my family contact me in an emergency?

The Peace Corps' Office of Special Services provides assistance in handling emergencies affecting trainees and Volunteers or their families. Before leaving the United States, instruct your family to notify the Office of Special Services immediately if an emergency arises, such as a serious illness or death of a family member. During normal business hours, the number for the Office of Special Services is 800.424.8580; select option 2, then extension 1470. After normal business hours and on weekends and holidays, the Special Services duty officer can be reached at the above number. For non-emergency questions, your family can get information from your country desk staff at the Peace Corps by calling 800.424.8580, extension 2519, 2520, or 2521.

Can I call home from Honduras?

International phone service to and from Honduras is relatively good. Hondutel, the local telephone agency, has offices in many cities and towns, and some of these offices offer direct lines to U.S. long-distance carriers. Most Volunteers make and receive international calls on their cellphones. Many Internet cafes also offer international phone lines from which you can make calls.

Should I bring a cellular phone with me?

No. You may buy one in Honduras. Phone cards are readily available.

Will there be email and Internet access?
Should I bring my computer?

There are a growing number of Internet cafes in urban centers throughout Honduras. Volunteers receive a monthly allowance for Internet use and are encouraged to utilize businesses in or near their communities. Volunteers do not have access to the equipment used by Peace Corps staff. If you choose to bring a laptop computer to Honduras, please take extra precautions as they are subject to theft and damage. If you choose to bring a laptop or other valuable equipment, you should insure it against theft and water damage.

Do Volunteers have diplomatic status during their service in Honduras?

No. Volunteers do not have diplomatic status, nor are they employees of the Peace Corps. They are subject to Honduran law and Peace Corps rules and regulations, and the U.S. Embassy cannot interfere with any judicial process.

WELCOME LETTERS FROM
HONDURAS VOLUNTEERS

Dear Prospective Volunteer,

Congratulations on your invitation to Peace Corps/Honduras. Your adventure awaits! I wish I could do it all over again. Volunteer work can be extremely challenging, but fulfilling. Sometimes it takes a lot of patience and a stick-to-it attitude. Here's my story:

I worked with a nongovernmental organization (NGO) that delivers filtration technology to improve rural communities' access to clean drinking water. My primary responsibilities were to train project personnel in organizational and technical skills and to strategically restructure the health program. These objectives were difficult due to a number of obstacles, including the limited high school education of my colleagues and working with an all-male team in a male-dominant culture.

It took many months to establish credibility with my counterparts as a "technical water and health consultant." For the first few months, I worked on small projects—improving the filter monitoring and anti-parasite programs, which were already in place but had not been optimized for efficiency. After six months, I designed an interactive hygiene education and filter review package for schoolchildren. My teammate, who has a penchant for lively discussion and teaching, designed a socio-drama that enjoyed great success as part of the hygiene training. One year into my service, a globally respected water purification consulting organization suggested we implement a volunteer training program to increase monitoring of filter use and project sustainability. We jumped on it. My counterpart and I created a training package to teach filter technology fundamentals and troubleshooting, and to establish a community-based monitoring network. At first, it was difficult to squeeze in an extra training day per community into our schedule, but once we began to see the positive results and community enthusiasm, it quickly became incorporated into the project.

Two years later, my teammates successfully use the computer for record keeping and planning and perform microbiology analyses. The hygiene and community volunteer education programs have now been integrated into the project lifecycle. Just two months post implementation; we trained 36 community volunteers in 14 rural communities to monitor filter use and advocate good hygiene, serving 3,000 beneficiaries. These programs were so successful that projects throughout the country have adopted them. I felt proudest when my organization conducted its first community volunteer training by itself. I know that this program will continue into the future, improving health and hygiene and positively impacting the lives of Hondurans long after the organization is gone.

Key things to remember: be patient, get to know people (relationships are very important), and enjoy yourself. I wish you a wonderful two years of service, challenge, and new friendships!

Dear Prospective Peace Corps Honduras Volunteers,

Congratulations! ¡Y Bienvenidos a Honduras! I remember getting my welcome packet and being excited, but not really having a clue as to what to expect. I have now been in my site for a year and am so glad I made the decision to join Peace Corps. As a health Volunteer, I support the local office of the NGO, World Vision, working with them in the campo with an indigenous population on a variety of health education topics. A lot of the time, I give talks and workshops on basic hygiene, nutrition, and reproductive health. I am also working on building a community garden for pregnant mothers at the maternal home, a place where women can go and stay near the hospital before giving birth. In addition to the work I do in my town, I am helping to develop some of the

Peace Corps/Honduras national initiatives, particularly in women's health. As part of the research for this initiative, I have had the opportunity to meet with heads of programs in agencies like USAID and the Ministry of Health. Peace Corps has opened new and exciting doors for me, in addition to making me think about what I want out of life.

I really enjoy the work I do, although, of course, at times it's frustrating and seemingly inconsequential. Meetings always start late, if at all, and often planned events will fall through—especially during rainy season. But I've learned to take it in stride and realized that the relationships I have built, and the process of learning more about myself, can be equally important. I've learned that I love being in my house, cooking dinner, having people over, or talking with my neighbors. Or eating fresh tortillas made just for me in a stranger's smoky kitchen. Ahh … such small joys.

One thing I would have never expected was to be in the comfort of my new home, with a cellphone, cable TV, and writing this letter to you on my laptop. At the same time, I am always aware that the electricity can go out at any minute and I might not have water tomorrow. You just never know. So here's my one bit of advice for those who want it: don't have expectations, be flexible, and have a good sense of humor.

Dear Prospective Volunteer,

Congratulations! I bet you are very excited right now, and you are very lucky to receive an invitation to come to Honduras. There are a lot of Volunteers, opportunities, and a long-standing and functional relationship between the Peace Corps and Honduras. This is the formal information you need to know, but what you really want is what to expect.

Becoming a Peace Corps Volunteer is rewarding and amazing, yet still a difficult experience. When I arrived at my site, I fell in love with it immediately. I knew that there would be work to do, even though, for the first month, I hadn't yet found most of it. I just kept showing up every day, talking to counterparts and sitting in the office, hoping to meet people. After building *confianza* with the people here, convincing them I really was here to stay and I was genuine in my desire to work and help the community, ideas and projects started coming in.

Another great thing about being a Volunteer is that you often end up doing different work than you expected to do and completing projects you did not believe you were capable of doing. Not that everything is perfect. There are always cancelled meetings; work that falls through; and hopes you have, only to discover that the community is not interested. But I have learned not to focus on these other than as a learning experience for next time, and to focus on the things that go well and grow into bigger projects, as well as the personal relationships you make on the way and the way living in another country just generally changes your life. Every site is different, but I have found that Volunteers who keep a positive attitude can laugh when things go differently than expected, and are genuine in their desire to help their community have an overall good experience in their sites.

What can I tell you about this beautiful country? You will need a lot of patience. Things will always be a little bit later or slower than you want them to be at first. But with time, you notice that you like the fact that life is a bit calmer and that things falling through is not the end of the world, like it can feel in the States. Often, a cancelled meeting or class can be a great opportunity to talk and meet people instead. You will build stronger relationships, which will help the meeting take place the next time around. This country is diverse. You can have a cold rainy mountain site, flat hot southern site, the northern beach, and anything in between.

Municipal development Volunteers work with mayors; community organizations, such as water boards; rural banks; business centers; schools; and nongovernmental organizations. The great thing is, you will be matched in a place that can use your skills and you can work with any of the above mentioned groups and create, with community partners, what is best for your town.

I remember how excited, yet scared, I was to come. I was worried about host families, making friends, surviving in Spanish, and so much more. But I have found the people here generally friendly and open and that it is a country that is patient with someone learning the language. We also have a large community of Volunteers, so there will be someone you will meet in this group who will help you get through the bad days as well, which we all have. Good luck over the next few weeks, and we look forward to having you here in Honduras!

PACKING LIST

This list has been compiled by Volunteers serving in Honduras and is based on their experience. Use it as an informal guide in making your own list, bearing in mind that each experience is individual. There is no perfect list! You obviously cannot bring everything on the list, so consider those items that make the most sense to you personally and professionally. You can always have things sent to you later. As you decide what to bring, keep in mind that you have an 80-pound weight limit on baggage. And remember, you can get almost everything you need in Honduras.

When packing, keep in mind that there are many products available in Honduras, but not necessarily in the pre-service training towns, with a few *pulperias* (local convenience stores) where you can purchase a limited and random supply of toiletries and school supplies. In Tegucigalpa and other bigger cities, there are malls and supermarkets where you can get all your products, down to a desired name brand, if you wish (bearing in mind that you'll be paying a bit more). That being said, it is best to bring enough of your favorite essentials for your time during training. You will not have time to visit Tegucigalpa during training to get a missing item. Nevertheless, know that you can buy them after you are in your site. In other words, you don't need to bring a two-year supply of anything, except for very specific and hard-to-find items or brands.

Another good rule of thumb is to leave at home anything that would make you really upset to lose. You may lose items through misplacing them, having them stolen, or simple breakage through wear-and-tear in this environment. Also, many Volunteers like to give away items to other Volunteers when they leave (because they do not want to travel with them). Thus, it is best to bring functional, yet cheap items.

Regarding clothing, pack to make yourself comfortable, but be prepared to dress in a way that is appropriate to the culture and your status as a professional. Women in particular will want to take care to avoid calling unwanted attention to themselves through their dress. This does not mean that women cannot wear things they would normally wear in the States, such as tank tops, but they will be expected to use their judgment to determine the most appropriate and culturally sensitive attire for the situation.

In addition, please be aware that the following suggestions of what to pack have been compiled by current and past Volunteers in Honduras. Your list will vary according to your personal preferences and comfort levels. You should bring what you feel you need and what you can easily carry. You will most likely be washing your clothes by hand, so clothes that are made from thin, light, and/or fast drying materials are recommended.

General Clothing

During training (as a trainee and Volunteer), you will be expected to wear "professional" clothing, which in Honduras loosely translates to business casual wear. For instance, collared short-sleeved and golf shirts, khakis or skirts are acceptable. Jeans that are not torn or ragged may be worn. It is fine to bring clothes that need to be ironed, because people here are quite meticulous about ironing their clothes and dressing neatly. Your host family will most likely have an iron to use. Later, depending on your site, you will probably be wearing the same business casual wear. Keep in mind, however, that in more rural sites, dress is very important, and even hard laborers will be seen wearing collared dress shirts, so you may want to bring one or two. Also, regarding weather, sites in Honduras range from extremely hot to extremely cool, so it is difficult to plan until you reach you're assigned community after training. The initial training site is in a rather cool climate, so you will want to be prepared with layers, and a jacket can come in handy. Expect to dress for fall in the training community. In general, it is best to bring a good mix of both cold weather and warm weather essentials, since, regardless of the weather at your site, you will most likely be traveling to various parts of the country. In addition, please note that there are an abundance of used clothing stores (*Ropa Americana*), where you can buy good-quality clothing at a very reasonable price. Most likely you will purchase something here, or you can get clothes made, sometime during your service since your clothes will get worn out more quickly here than in the States.

In short, you will be able to purchase plenty of inexpensive clothing in-country, so just bring the essentials to get you through training. A more detailed list follows:

- Five pair of nice pants/skirts/jeans (two weeks' worth); skirts and dresses should be no shorter than knee length
- Seven business casual shirts (two weeks' worth)
- Two long-sleeve breathable cotton shirts
- One long-sleeved hooded sweatshirt/light sweater/light fleece (quick-dry fabric recommended)
- One collared dress shirt
- One tie for men for the swearing-in ceremony
- One pair of semiformal dress/shoes to match for women for swearing-in ceremony
- Two weeks' worth of cotton underwear
- Ten pairs of cotton socks
- One pair of wool socks (also can be used as slippers to walk around inside)
- Three to four comfortable bras and one or two sports bras
- Two pajama bottoms
- Three pajama T-shirts
- One casual, comfortable outfit for going out
- A couple pairs of long shorts or capris that reach to mid-calf

Rain gear: You will need a light, breathable rain jacket/windbreaker/poncho for the downpours during the rainy season. Also, a small travel umbrella is convenient for protection from the rain and sun, as used by many Honduran women. If your site is rainy and muddy enough for rubber boots, you can always purchase them at the markets in bigger cities, so bringing them is unnecessary.

Bathing suit: Generally, people here wear T-shirts and shorts to go swimming, sometimes with a bathing suit underneath, but there are enough opportunities to go swimming to merit bringing whatever type of bathing suit you like. You may want to bring swim shorts or board shorts as well. Women may also want to consider bringing a more conservative suit for use in and near their site, and another they would use on vacation.

Shoes

Sandals: A good, comfy pair of sturdy sandals for everyday wear is a must. Also, you will need a cheap pair of flip-flops for shower shoes. These can be found easily in Honduras. Nice sandals can be considered business casual wear, but do not expect to wear flip-flop style sandals during training, in the Peace Corps office, or when you are at work.

Hiking/mountain/all-terrain boots: Much of the terrain in Honduras is very irregular, which means that supportive hiking shoes are convenient for long walks or even just to wear as your everyday footwear. Volunteers like to use waterproof shoes since they can be a lifesaver during the rainy season, but remember that they are a little less breathable than non-waterproof shoes. Good quality waterproof boots are hard to find here so you may want to consider purchasing these stateside. Sizes larger than 9 are hard to find for any type of shoe.

Sneakers/running shoes: Depending on your preference, you can either bring the aforementioned hiking boots or a good pair of sneakers (or both if you use them for different purposes). Quality sneakers can usually be found in Tegucigalpa and San Pedro Sula, but they are expensive.

Comfortable dress shoes: Although you will most likely be wearing sandals or sneakers in your site, it is necessary to have a pair of dress shoes for training and/or dressier events that you may need to attend during service. Dress shoes, in general, translate to comfortable closed-toed shoes. Keep in mind that dust runs rampant in Honduras, so it is best to bring a pair that will endure this environment.

Personal Hygiene and Toiletry Items

Personal hygiene items: This may include anti-bacterial hand gel in travel sizes and stain-removing wipes (e.g., Shout Wipes). Don't overload, we do have soap in Honduras. Also consider a fabric pen, a good nail care set and tweezers, a brush/comb, a toothbrush and travel toothbrush case, hair clippers (men), and for women, your favorite brand of tampons to last you through training. Also, if there is any sort of specific, nice-quality hygiene items that you use regularly (e.g., body lotions, hair products, oil-free sunscreen), you may want to bring these to make your life more comfortable. Most people find that the local products are just fine and that they can live without a lot of "essentials" after a few weeks.

Miscellaneous

Bath towel: You can buy smaller, cheaper-quality, quick drying bath towels in Honduras. Many Volunteers bring one large towel with them to use during training and throughout service. You may find a quick-dry towel, like the kind you can buy in camping stores, helpful, especially in the cool training site and during the rainy season.

Medium-sized backpack: A lot of people have made the mistake of bringing large expedition backpacks, with nothing for day-to-day use or a weekend trip. No matter what the size, packs with zippered side pockets are great and will always be useful. Current Volunteers recommend bringing both a large and day pack. It's a good idea if this travel backpack isn't flashy, as you will use it often to travel on buses. An even smaller over-the-shoulder bag that you can carry daily can be useful.

Pocket knife or Leatherman: This is always convenient to have, even if it's only as an extra knife or can opener in the kitchen.

Work Gloves: In virtually any project you will want a pair of gloves for outside work.

Durable AA flashlight or headlamp (LED): While most sites have electricity, it often is unreliable and inconsistent, periodically going out for hours or even days. Thus, a sturdy flashlight (e.g., Maglite) or headlamp (perfect for hands-free cooking) is essential.

Battery re-charger (AA): Batteries here are expensive, low quality, and (as anywhere) horrible for the environment. So, it is recommended to bring a battery re-charger according to the size of batteries required by whatever electronics you bring with you. Also, two to three sets of rechargeable batteries are recommended. Some Volunteers solely use batteries due to the power outages that can ruin appliances, or because they don't have electricity. However, even if your site does not have electricity, you will have access to areas that do (e.g., the capital, your closest city or *pueblo*), so you will still be able to plug in an electric re-charger at some point.

One or two durable water bottles: Many Volunteers like hard plastic water bottles because they are so tough. Re-using plastic water bottles is another option.

Travel sewing kit: Clothes go through a rougher time here than they do in the States, especially during washing, and a sewing kit becomes necessary more often.

A camera: People in your site will love to see the instantaneous display of a digital camera, and digital photos are easier to send home or just burn onto a CD. As with expensive valuables, it's a good idea to insure your camera before arrival.

Watch/Travel Alarm Clock: You should bring a small clock that does not need electricity, and that will wake you up. This is especially convenient for early training days.

A money belt: Most people feel safer with one to hide their money when traveling.

Sleep sac or light sleeping bag: You'll do some overnight traveling during training to visit other Volunteers' sites, and you never know what kind of accommodations will be available. Thus, you need to have something to sleep on. Blankets or larger items are not recommended because it's better to wait and assess your needs once you arrive at your site and then buy bulky items in-country as necessary. A light sleeping bag is perfect for traveling and in-site use. (Make sure it is light so it is practical for the weather in Honduras)

Sunglasses: This sunny country can do major harm to your eyes. Bring a cheap pair of sunglasses; flashy ones are too tempting for thieves. You can always buy a replacement pair in-country.

Personal photos: These are not only great for the occasional pick-me-up, but also to show your host family and the folks in your site. People love seeing these photos, and they are a good way to practice your Spanish and develop relationships.

A small CD player/MP3 player/radio: Many Volunteers bring portable CD players or radios and then attach small speakers to turn them into stereos. However, you can also buy a stereo in-country if needed. Remember that electronics can be extremely expensive here, with a huge mark-up on the prices found in the U.S. The terrain here makes a shortwave radio useless in many parts of the country, so a simple radio is your best option. If you bring a laptop, consider bringing small external speakers, as your laptop could become your entertainment center.

Portable USB memory drive: As this technology becomes more common, most Volunteers in Honduras have brought these with them or had one sent. Regardless of whether you have a personal computer or computer available at your site, there are plenty of instances where a memory drive comes in handy. You can use them at

Internet cafes, fellow Volunteers' sites, and the Volunteer-designated computers at the Peace Corps office to transfer information and resources easily and safely (especially reports) and to trade photos and music. Bring two!

Surge protector and uninterruptible power supply (also known as voltage stabilizer) for your electronics: The inconsistent electricity in Honduras is harmful to most electronics. While you may find these items in larger stores in Honduras, you will not be able to easily get them during training.

Non-Essentials, but Nice if You Don't Mind Carrying It

Laptop computer: Some Volunteers have reservations about bringing laptops due to security, maintenance, and use issues. Current Volunteers, however, highly recommend bringing your personal laptop or netbook. Many Volunteers who bring laptops feel they have been most useful. If you choose to bring one, a basic laptop is sufficient, with the basic Microsoft programs (i.e., Excel, Word, Access) or their equivalent. It may facilitate your work, especially if you don't have a computer available at your counterpart agency's office. At the same time, you should consider if/how you will ensure that work you accomplish on your laptop and if it can be transferred to your counterpart agency. Laptops are convenient for downloading digital photos, watching DVDs, listening to music, playing games, and reviewing resources available on CD-ROMs. Many Volunteers even use laptops to write emails at home, save them, and then spend less money to just send them once they reach an Internet café. If you do not have electricity in your site, most laptops have a battery that can last for a good amount of time. If you do decide to bring a laptop, you should always insure expensive items in case of theft or breakage. In addition, the dusty and humid atmosphere may cause maintenance problems with your laptop, which are difficult to fix in-country. Current Volunteers strongly recommend you insure your equipment since a number of laptops have been stolen when Volunteers' residences have been burglarized or when they have been traveling by bus. Apple computers can be hard to get repaired in Honduras.

External hard drive: If you do decide to bring your laptop, you may want to consider bringing an external hard drive as well. Current Volunteers highly recommend an external hard drive to both share information and to back up your computer. A normal laptop's life expectancy is shortened even further by the dust and heat of many Honduran sites. Because of security concerns, it is also a good idea to have everything backed up and stored separately from your computer.

Hobby kit/activities: Volunteers bring yoga kits, books, magnetic chess/checker boards, decks of cards, travel games, word puzzles, etc. —all of which can be used for your personal time and with people in your site, both for fun and for incorporating your educational information. If you enjoy sports, bring your gear (your baseball glove, cleats, Frisbee, your workout clothes, or other small, lightweight supplies). If you plan on bringing your laptop, you may want to download a few entertaining games.

Travel coffee/tea mug: These are especially great during training. Although you can find any type of coffee here, if you enjoy tea, bring a couple boxes of your favorite kinds because there are only about three varieties available in-country.

Sleeping mat: These are not essential because you can buy cheap, thin mattresses for guests in most sites, or just sleep on a bunch of blankets when traveling. However, some Volunteers love their sleeping mats (or even yoga mats) and bring them wherever they go.

Travel pillow: This is not a necessity, but some people use them for bus rides. Consider an inflatable pillow you can wrap around your neck.

Stationary supplies: Plain paper is available here, but if you like nice letter-writing supplies, they can be hard to find. You can find pens, pencils, and markers, but you might want to bring a few to get you through training.

Makeup/jewelry/accessories: It's not a good idea to bring anything flashy, especially gold, and you should only bring things you would feel comfortable wearing in the States and that you wouldn't mind losing.

Gift for host family: Many Volunteers like to bring something representative of their home region to give to their host families. You will have two different families during pre-service training and then a third when you move to your new site. However, other Volunteers feel awkward giving gifts upon arrival and either wait until the end of their stay to give the gift they brought, or just purchase something useful for the host family in-country after getting to know them (e.g., coffee, calendar, home goods, treats for kids, crayons, playing cards).

Re-sealable plastic bags: These help keep little pests from getting into food and keep food fresh in the humidity. Plastic bags can be also used for traveling with toiletries to avoid spillage.

Warm cap/scarf: If you get chilly easily, bring something to cover your head for cold mornings during training. You will not be able to find these items in your training site. However, remember that you can find scarves and/or hats in-country if you are placed in a site with a cool climate.

A few good books. The Peace Corps office in Tegucigalpa has an informal library for Volunteers, which contains a wide range of titles that have been circulating among Volunteers over the years. While there is never a shortage of books (since people are always donating and returning new ones), some Volunteers find the available books to be old and uninteresting. Though you will always be able to find something to read if you have a good eye and dig deep enough, those with particular tastes should bring a few books to occupy their time and then find some good friends with whom they can trade.

What NOT to Bring

Medical supplies: All the medical supplies you could possibly need are available here through the Peace Corps. The health care for Volunteers is excellent. All Volunteers receive a medical kit at the close of pre-service training. The medical office will provide you with refills of everything in the kit. This includes bug spray, sun block, lip protector, floss, condoms, cough drops, cold medicines, stomach medicines, bandages, mosquito net, and many other items. Women receive plastic applicator tampons from the medical unit since they are difficult to find in-country. Sanitary pads are easily purchased throughout Honduras. If you are comfortable using these, you do not need to bring your own supplies (**except those that you will need for the first three months of training**). If you prefer a specific type or brand of tampons, you should bring them with you. **A note on tampons:** several female Volunteers have purchased a product called the "Diva Cup," which is an environmentally friendly alternative to tampons and/or sanitary pads. It is especially helpful if you serve in a site where you will have to burn your trash. Remember to bring your own prescription medicines for your first three to six months in-country.

Tool kits: Volunteers in the past have brought tools such as hammers and screwdrivers and found them unnecessary. You can usually borrow these items from a neighbor or landlord if necessary. If you absolutely need your own, you can buy these items for cheap prices at hardware stores in most towns.

Bedding: Your host families must provide bedding. And, until you arrive in your site, you will not know what size of bed you will need to be given or buy. Thus, it is best to just buy sheets at a market, and perhaps use your sleep sac for the first few nights before purchasing sheets. If you are particular about sheets, those found here are low quality, so you may consider having these sent to you.

Kitchen supplies: You can find all of these in local markets or malls in larger cities.

Cellphone: You will be able to buy one in Honduras at a reasonable price.

Iron: You do not need to bring one. You may borrow or buy one in-country.

Outdoor "survival" gear: Although you are going to live in a developing country, please remember that the Peace Corps will never place you in a site where a minimum standard of living is not possible. Unless you use them often in the States, or if you plan on taking a jungle trip (and even then, most trips provide gear), it is unnecessary to bring water pumps/purifiers (you can boil your water or use iodine tablets), tents (however, a tent would be good if you are a passionate hiker), compasses, binoculars, etc. However, if you are an avid outdoors person, these items may be essential to you so you should bring them since you will not be able to buy them in Honduras.

As a final note, remember not to bring too many products because you can find nearly everything you could possibly want here. It is amazing how much Volunteers acquire in their two years of living in Honduras. A good rule of thumb is to bring half of what you think you'll need. Packing can be a pain, but hopefully this will make it easier. And, don't stress out: things can always be sent to you from the States.

PRE-DEPARTURE CHECKLIST

The following list consists of suggestions for you to consider as you prepare to live outside the United States for two years. Not all items will be relevant to everyone, and the list does not include everything you should make arrangements for.

Family

- Notify family that they can call the Peace Corps' Office of Special Services at any time if there is a critical illness or death of a family member (24-hour telephone number: 800.424.8580, extension 1470).

- Give the Peace Corps' *On the Home Front* handbook to family and friends.

Passport/Travel

- Forward to the Peace Corps travel office all paperwork for the Peace Corps passport and visas.

- Verify that your luggage meets the size and weight limits for international travel.

- Obtain a personal passport if you plan to travel after your service ends. (Your Peace Corps passport will expire three months after you finish your service, so if you plan to travel longer, you will need a regular passport.)

Medical/Health

- Complete any needed dental and medical work.

- If you wear glasses, bring two pairs.

- Arrange to bring a three-month supply of all medications (including birth control pills) you are currently taking.

Insurance

- Make arrangements to maintain life insurance coverage.

- Arrange to maintain supplemental health coverage while you are away. (Even though the Peace Corps is responsible for your health care during Peace Corps service overseas, it is advisable for people who have pre-existing conditions to arrange for the continuation of their supplemental health coverage. If there is a lapse in coverage, it is often difficult and expensive to be reinstated.)

- Arrange to continue Medicare coverage if applicable.

Personal Papers

- Bring a copy of your certificate of marriage or divorce.

Voting

- Register to vote in the state of your home of record. (Many state universities consider voting and payment of state taxes as evidence of residence in that state.)

- Obtain a voter registration card and take it with you overseas.

- Arrange to have an absentee ballot forwarded to you overseas.

Personal Effects

- Purchase personal property insurance to extend from the time you leave your home for service overseas until the time you complete your service and return to the United States.

Financial Management

- Keep a bank account in your name in the U.S.

- Obtain student loan deferment forms from the lender or loan service.

- Execute a Power of Attorney for the management of your property and business.

- Arrange for deductions from your readjustment allowance to pay alimony, child support, and other debts through the Office of Volunteer Financial Operations at 800.424.8580, extension 1770.

- Place all important papers—mortgages, deeds, stocks, and bonds—in a safe deposit box or with an attorney or other caretaker.

CONTACTING PEACE CORPS HEADQUARTERS

This list of numbers will help connect you with the appropriate office at Peace Corps headquarters to answer various questions. You can use the toll-free number and extension or dial directly using the local numbers provided. Be sure to leave the toll-free number and extensions with your family so they can contact you in the event of an emergency.

Peace Corps Headquarters Toll-free Number: 800.424.8580, Press 2, Press 1, then Ext. # (see below)

Peace Corps' Mailing Address: Peace Corps
Paul D. Coverdell Peace Corps Headquarters
1111 20th Street, NW
Washington, DC 20526

For Questions About:	Staff:	Toll-Free Ext:	Direct/Local Number:
Responding to an Invitation:			
	Office of Placement	x1840	202.692.1840
Country Information	Lori Wallace	x2519	202.692.2519
	Desk Officer /	lwallace@peacecorps.gov	
Plane Tickets, Passports, Visas, or other travel matters:			
	SATO Travel	x1170	202.692.1170
Legal Clearance	Office of Placement	x1840	202.692.1840
Medical Clearance and Forms Processing (includes dental):			
	Screening Nurse	x1500	202.692.1500
Medical Reimbursements (handled by a subcontractor)			800.818.8772
Loan Deferments, Taxes, Financial Operations		x1770	202.692.1770
Readjustment Allowance Withdrawals, Power of Attorney, Staging (Pre-Departure Orientation), and Reporting Instructions:			
	Office of Staging	x1865	202.692.1865

Note: You will receive comprehensive information (hotel and flight arrangements three to five weeks prior to departure. This information is not available sooner.

Family Emergencies (to get information to a Volunteer overseas) *24 hours:*

	Office of Special	x1470	202.692.1470

www.ingramcontent.com/pod-product-compliance
Lightning Source LLC
Chambersburg PA
CBHW080448290526
45791CB00008BA/2648